D1414879

Stepping Into the Light

*The Miraculous Ways That Our Loved Ones,
Angels & Guides Are Able To Let Us Know They Are Near*

JULIA TREAT

BALBOA.
PRESS
A DIVISION OF HAY HOUSE

Balboa Press books may be ordered through booksellers or by contacting:

Balboa Press
A Division of Hay House
1663 Liberty Drive
Bloomington, IN 47403
www.balboapress.com
1 (877) 407-4847

Because of the dynamic nature of the Internet, any web addresses or links contained in this book may have changed since publication and may no longer be valid. The views expressed in this work are solely those of the author and do not necessarily reflect the views of the publisher, and the publisher hereby disclaims any responsibility for them.

The author of this book does not dispense medical advice or prescribe the use of any technique as a form of treatment for physical, emotional, or medical problems without the advice of a physician, either directly or indirectly. The intent of the author is only to offer information of a general nature to help you in your quest for emotional and spiritual well-being. In the event you use any of the information in this book for yourself, which is your constitutional right, the author and the publisher assume no responsibility for your actions.

Any people depicted in stock imagery provided by Thinkstock are models, and such images are being used for illustrative purposes only.
Certain stock imagery © Thinkstock.

Print information available on the last page.

ISBN: 978-1-5043-3306-1 (sc)
ISBN: 978-1-5043-3308-5 (hc)
ISBN: 978-1-5043-3307-8 (e)

Library of Congress Control Number: 2015907706

Balboa Press rev. date: 5/26/2015

To all of my loved ones, angels, and guides who have been a part of my amazing journey: I thank you for helping me embrace my destiny. I not only understand the unconditional love that you hold for me, I also feel it each and every day. Thank you for holding my heart in your hands. To my amazing mentor and coach, Jackie Eaton, who I hold so close to my heart. You have been an amazing blessing in my life, and I am eternally grateful for your wisdom and guidance. Thank you for all that you do. You freaking rock!

Contents

Introduction

This book was not written to convince anyone of anything. It was written merely to perhaps help you tap into your own consciousness and awaken what your soul already knows to be true, that the universe is limitless and that love—and only love—is the answer to everything.

This book is the culmination of several years I've spent on an amazing spiritual journey. Its manifestation is the result of my long and sometimes difficult journey of facing and overcoming so many of my own doubts and fears. Thanks to my amazing guides in heaven as well as several here on earth, I am finally able to step away from the fears that have controlled my life for far too long. It is with great passion, love, and gratitude that I share my story with you. As the saying goes, "The truth will set you free." I am finally free.

This book is divided into two parts. The first half is about my own personal journey into the world of being able to communicate with the realms above. My story is filled with amazing events and "coincidences" that had to occur to get me to where I am today. There are several unique and surprising stories of how I connected with different beings such as angels, spirit guides, and departed loved ones. The second half is full of more amazing stories from many of my clients and the miraculous ways that their loved ones, angels, and guides were able to let them know they were near. Some of their stories just may blow you away! I share all of these experiences with you in the hopes that they may help you realize the unlimited possibilities that await you. May you remember the light that exists within, that connects us all. May you open up to the unlimited possibilities that are waiting just for you. May you step into your power and embrace your destiny with grace and ease.

*Some of the names in this book have been changed out of respect for my clients and to protect their identities. I am grateful for those who allowed me to share their amazing stories so that others might be able to realize all that is possible.

PART I

My Awakening

Chapter 1

The Preacher's Daughter

As the daughter of a Baptist minister, I had always been taught about God's love and grace. I grew up in the church and took part in just about every activity possible, whether it was playing the piano during church service, participating in youth group, or going to church camp. My father was, and still is, an amazing minister and will always be my biggest role model. I have always admired his faith and conviction, and although there were plenty of times when it would've seemed appropriate, I have never seen it waiver. I brag about him often and tell people that for all of his good deeds, he will reach some sort of sainthood when he gets to heaven. It amazes me to this day that I have never heard my father say anything negative about anyone, and believe me, there were plenty of opportunities where most would say it was warranted.

My father taught me so much, but most of all, he taught me to always help others to the best of my ability. While growing up in South Dakota, I can remember the never-ending phone calls my father would receive. I would often accompany him on visits with shut-ins and to nursing homes, and I would also help him work with the many homeless people in our area. I was always the first one to volunteer to go along when my dad received calls of someone in distress. Some of these souls were individuals who were down on their luck and needed a good meal and a place to sleep. I can't recall the number of times my father took money out of his own pocket to pay for food and shelter for a complete stranger. Occasionally, he would get a call about someone drunk and passed out on the street. One of those calls stands out in my mind.

My dad received a call about a gentleman who was passed out on the side of the road after drinking too much alcohol. I'm not certain of my age but remember being quite young at the time, probably around six or seven. I asked my dad if I could go along, and he didn't hesitate in saying yes. Back then, maybe it wasn't as dangerous as it is these days, but then again, I'm sure my father felt completely protected, as he knew he was doing God's work. I was always eager to spend time with my dad, and I just couldn't wait to go help someone in need. As our car turned down the street where the man was supposed to be, it didn't take long to spot him. He was an older gentleman with a large build, and he was lying slumped over next to an empty bottle of rubbing alcohol. At the time, that was the drink of choice for many in the area who were financially distressed, and unfortunately, these types of calls weren't out of the ordinary. My father parked next to the gentleman and got out of the car. He walked over to the man, placed his hand on his shoulder, and gently woke him up. He told the gentleman that we were going to take him somewhere where he could get a hot meal and a bed for the night. Although the man was still out of sorts a bit, he was definitely grateful for my father's kind words. I will never forget the smell that permeated our car when that man got in. It will be imbedded in my mind for eternity.

I remember sitting in the back seat and wondering if he had any family or friends. *Doesn't anyone care about him?* I thought as we drove to the shelter. As usual, my father spoke with the man with such love and compassion. He was never judgmental and always wanted to make sure that whomever he was helping knew that someone cared. We arrived at the shelter, and my father walked the gentleman to the door. He reached out and shook the man's hand and leaned over and said, "I'll keep you in my prayers." I can assure you that he did.

That man was just one of many that received a helping hand from my dad. I am so grateful that my father taught me the true meaning of unconditional love and compassion and how important it is to offer those things to others. They have been the driving force in all that I do.

I can only hope that I will leave this world a better place, as I know that he has. I will always remember my father as a loving and compassionate person, willing to help anyone in need. He was always so full of love and light, and I feel honored to have been his daughter.

Chapter 2

Connecting with Angels

I received my master of arts degree in speech-language pathology in 2003 from the University of Kansas, and I pursued a career helping children and adults with speech, language, and feeding disorders. As a speech pathologist, we're required to earn continuing education hours, and although I had earned some of my hours close to home, I would occasionally travel to different destinations if someone was teaching something I was interested in. One day, I stumbled across a course in Colorado that seemed quite interesting. It was different than anything I had ever taken before, and I was always eager to learn new things. I signed up for the course and booked a flight for the following month. Although the course was absolutely amazing, I know that I was guided to take it for a much bigger reason. While attending, I met one of the kindest and most loving people I have ever met. Barbara was an earth angel in every sense of the word. She had such a beauty about her that just couldn't be explained. You could feel the love that flowed from her heart as soon as she entered the room. I was supposed to go to Colorado so that I could be introduced to the angels.

One evening after class, Barb and I met for dinner. I don't recall a lot of details about our conversation, but I know that we started talking about angels. Barb started talking about how the angels had helped her change her life in such amazing ways. I was mesmerized as she talked about the different angels, their names, and what they were able to help with. Barb asked me if I wanted to stop by her hotel room to continue our conversation. I was happy to and couldn't wait to hear more. Barb and I were staying at the same hotel and just so happened to be right down the hall from one another. After stopping at my room for a quick change into some comfy clothes, I ventured down to Barbara's room. When I arrived, Barb walked over to her nightstand and grabbed a small box. She walked over to where I was sitting and placed it in my hands.

"These are my Archangel Oracle Cards I was talking about earlier," she said. I stared at the shiny pink and gold box. It had a beautiful angel on the front. "You're welcome to take these back to your room tonight if you want to, to see what the angels have to say to you," she said. I had no idea what they were, as I had never seen them before.

"What do I do with them?" I asked.

"Ask the angels any question and then pull out as many cards as you feel you should," she said. I'll have to admit, as soon as she put those cards in my hands, I couldn't wait to get back to my room to try them out. I was like a kid at Christmas.

"Thank you," I exclaimed as I hugged her tightly. "I can't wait to see what happens."

When I got back to my room, I quickly sat in the middle of my bed and opened the box. I took the cards out, gazing at each of them for a few moments. They were so beautiful. Each angel had a different name and came with a different message. I looked at each and every one of them in detail and began to feel something happening—some sort of connection was occurring. I had no idea exactly what was happening. I just knew that I felt like something was happening inside of me—like something that had been dormant for a very long time had suddenly been awakened.

I shuffled the cards, all forty-four of them, a few times and tried to think of a question. *Hmm,* I thought, *what can I ask?* Although it was probably just a minute or two, it seemed like forever. I couldn't think of anything to ask. *Aha! I'll ask about my life purpose.* I knew I had a burning desire to work with children and wanted to test the cards to see if they actually worked. I began thinking about my question: *Angels, what is my life purpose?* I continued shuffling the cards and remembered what Barbara had said, that I would just know when to stop. Just as she had told me, it happened. My hands stopped. It was time to pick my cards, and I was guided to pick three of them. Barb had told me to trust my intuition, and it was telling me to pick three cards from the top. I pulled the cards and laid them out facedown in front of me on the bed. I was so nervous and eager all at the same time. My heart was racing, and I didn't know why. I took a deep breath and turned the cards over one by one. I couldn't believe my eyes! The first card was a picture of an angel waving that said, "Hello from Heaven." The second card said, "All is well," and the third was a picture of an angel standing behind three children that read, "Indigo and crystal children."

Oh, shit! I thought. *This is crazy.* As I read the meaning of each card, I still couldn't believe what had just happened. I had asked about my life purpose, and the angels had given me a card with children on it. *Hmm,* I thought, *maybe I'll do it again just to make sure.* I stuck the three cards in the deck, making sure to place them in different places so they weren't next to one another. Still in some disbelief, I shuffled the cards for a bit and then said, "Angels, if this is for real, I want the same three cards." I couldn't believe what I was saying. I was basically telling the angels that I would only believe if they did same thing again. I wanted the same three cards in the same order. I shuffled longer than I had the first time and repeated my question. "Angels, what is my life purpose?" Just like the first time, I knew when to stop. I picked three cards from the top of the deck and laid them facedown in front of me. I was more nervous than I had been the first time! I took a deep breath and turned the cards over. They were the same three cards in the exact same order. I could not believe my eyes. I was overcome with emotion and just began sobbing. I can't explain the flood of emotion that came over me. It was an overwhelming feeling of love, and I knew, at that moment, that I had just connected with the angels. I cried so hard, but they were tears of love and joy. It was a feeling I'd never felt before, and I felt I was releasing a lifetime of pain and sorrow. I could feel so many angels around me, and I knew things would never be the same from that day on. There were so many angels, and they loved me!

The next day, I met Barb for class. I couldn't wait to tell her what had happened. I told her how the angels had given me the same exact three cards two times in a row. I told her how I had begun sobbing and that I had been so overcome with emotion. Barb just smiled as I told my story, and when I was finished, she simply replied, "You just had your first true connection with the angels."

She went on to say that people are often overcome with the same emotion that I felt when they reconnect with their angels.

"We all come into this world as infants, still connected to that amazing energy of God and the angels," she said. "Then, as we begin living our lives as humans, one fearful thought after another begins to block all that we know about that beautiful place (heaven). Last night, you returned to that space of true unconditional love, the love of the angels. They love you so much."

My eyes welled up with tears again as I listened to the earth angel standing right in front of me. I know she was an angel sent to help me on my journey, and I will be forever grateful for the gift she gave me.

When I returned home, I wasted no time ordering my own deck of Archangel cards. I couldn't wait to use them again and was eager to hear more from my new friends. I rushed the shipping, as I didn't want to be away from them for long. My cards came within a couple of days, and I began using them every single day. I would ask all sorts of questions, and they would answer with spot-on advice. I used them when I got up in the morning and before I went to bed each night. I felt so close to the angels, and that feeling only got stronger the more I used them. I began to feel the angels around me each day, and I could swear that something was starting to shift inside of me. I couldn't put my finger on it at the time but I knew that something was changing, and I knew that it was something I wanted more of.

As my bond with the angels grew stronger and stronger, I started calling on the angels to be with me each day and to guide me as I worked with my clients. At the time, I was working as a speech pathologist in several different settings. I had always been the type to get bored with something easily, and dividing my time among different settings, ages, and particular needs seemed to take care of that issue. Each day was different, and I looked forward to facing any challenges my clients faced, always striving to help them see the unlimited possibilities that waited for them. Besides providing therapy for elderly and ill patients in long-term-care facilities, I also enjoyed seeing children from birth to three years of age in their homes for early intervention. And if that wasn't enough, I began building a private practice in my home where I could see clients with all sorts of needs. I was a busy girl and loving every minute.

As I continued working closely with the angels using my oracle cards, I began buying books and online programs—anything that would teach me more about them. Although I had been raised in the church, I really didn't recall hearing much about the angels—the archangel Gabrielle announcing Jesus's birth and perhaps a few other stories, but that was just about the extent of it. I guess I had never really understood that there were so many of them until this new path had unfolded, and I certainly had no idea that some of them had "specialties." I was amazed at all of the new things I was learning about angels, and I just couldn't get enough. Life was good. I had everything I had ever dreamed of: an amazing career, a wonderful husband and marriage, a new home. I had it all. Or, at least, I thought I did. Little did I know that my whole life was about to be turned upside down. The beginning of my rock bottom was about to hit me square between the eyes, and I can assure you, I was not ready.

Chapter 3

My World Turned Upside Down

After 9/11, my husband expressed interest in going over to help with the war effort. He had been retired from the air force for a number of years and had already been retired for a couple of years when we met. It's funny; I remember telling him on our wedding day something along the lines of, "I'm not cut out to be a military wife." In hindsight, I can't help but wonder if that was my own intuition trying to give me a heads up.

As time passed, Scott's desire to head over to Afghanistan grew deeper and deeper. I found myself in tears even at the mention of it. As much as I tried to push it aside, it never went away. He would watch reports on television and I could see that there was some sort of burning desire to be over there with his comrades. His feelings seemed to get stronger and stronger, and the day I had always dreaded finally came. Scott told me that he needed to go "do his part." That he had such a strong feeling that he was supposed to go to Afghanistan. I knew he had been stationed overseas during his career in the air force, but that was before. Before he knew me. I was devastated and began sobbing. I begged him not to go and reminded him that we had just started our beautiful life together.

"I just got out of school and am building my career, you have a great job close to home, and we just bought this amazing new house," I pleaded. Although I tried desperately to convince him not to leave, I somehow knew it was something he just had to do. He notified his superiors and told them he was volunteering to go over to Afghanistan.

My heart sank. The love of my life was leaving to go halfway around the world to a place of death and destruction. I was terrified for him and found myself feeling abandoned, rejected, and completely alone. I was angry that he had decided to go, yet I held that in and sheltered him from my true feelings. Maybe if I would've started kicking and screaming and demanded that he not go, we would still be married. But even that wouldn't have stopped him, I'm sure. He was destined to go so that he could grow and learn whatever it was he needed to, as I would do the same in his absence. I know that now, but at the time, I felt totally lost. It was done. He had volunteered, and now all we had to do was wait. Wait for that dreadful day when we would have to say good-bye.

That day came six months later. It was time for Scott to go and there was nothing I could do. We drove to the airport and said our good-byes as tears flowed down both of our faces. I find tears welling up even now as I recall that horrible day. It's so difficult to find the words to express what was going on inside of me, but the pain was almost unbearable. As he boarded the plane that would take him to his new home for the next year, I felt as if a death had occurred. There was an emptiness in my heart that was like nothing I'd felt before. I watched his plane take off into the sunset and did the only thing I knew to do: I called on the angels and asked them to keep him safe.

With my husband halfway around the world, I found myself filling my days with as much activity as I could. I guess I wanted to make the time go by as quickly as possible and felt that if I kept busy, it might go by quicker somehow. I hired a personal trainer and began working out three days a week. I started painting the inside of our new home and enjoyed getting the space ready for our future. I worked diligently trying to build my private practice as I continued to work for different agencies. As I worked on building my private practice, I began to learn new modalities. I was always eager to learn and was excited to offer different things to my new and existing clients. I heard about a weekend course being held in Pennsylvania. The content being offered was right up my alley, so I signed up to attend and booked my flight. What I thought was yet another routine trip to learn some new things and receive some continuing education hours would actually become a huge turning point in my life.

By the time my trip to Pennsylvania rolled around, my husband had been gone for several months. Although we were able to talk often over the phone, my heart was still hurting terribly. I would put on a brave face as we talked about what was going on in our lives, but inside, I was gradually falling apart. I didn't want to say anything to him to upset him, as I knew he was in a far worse place than I was. I remember thinking how selfish it was of me to still feel so rejected and hurt, but it was the truth. And I was still angry that he had left in the first place. I obviously had a lot of stuff that I had to work through, but I guess I just wasn't ready to. I still wasn't able to find my voice and say exactly how I felt. That was a pattern that I seemed to have my entire life. I would never speak up and say exactly how I felt for fear of hurting someone else. Good grief, that really screwed things up, believe me.

It finally came time for my trip to Pennsylvania. I'd never been there before and couldn't wait to see something new. I remember being in awe as we passed over some of the most beautiful landscape I had ever seen. There were endless mountains with beautiful trees. It was fall and the leaves had recently begun to change, allowing the trees to show their amazing colors. It was absolutely breathtaking and reminded me of the hills of South Dakota, where I had grown up. Oh, how I missed the mountains. My plane landed, and I made my way to my hotel. I knew that several of my colleagues, whom I had met before, were attending the same conference, and I couldn't wait to spend time with them again. They were a fun and lively bunch, and I was in need of lots of joy and laughter. We found each other at the hotel and our fun-filled weekend began.

It was a decent-size conference with a couple hundred people in attendance. There were many familiar faces and lots of people that I didn't know. While attending the conference, I made some new friends who lived in northeastern Pennsylvania, smack-dab in the middle of the Endless Mountains. We became friends quickly, and they invited me up for a visit. I agreed and found myself booking a plane ticket within a few weeks to return. One trip turned into more. I began visiting

Pennsylvania periodically and found myself falling in love with the area. After the third trip or so, I began feeling a longing to go back and couldn't wait until I was able to visit again. I was drawn to the area for some reason, and at the time, I didn't really know why. Yes, it was beautiful and reminded me of South Dakota, but the pull to go there seemed like it was about so much more than that. I didn't realize it at the time, but the universe was getting me ready for some major shifts— shifts that would bring me to where I am today.

As the time grew near for my husband to return home, I found myself getting so excited. My feelings were similar to how I felt when we first started dating. I was full of excitement and eager for us to be together once again. We had continued our weekly phone calls, but nothing could compare to being in each other's arms. Oh, how I couldn't wait to begin our life together. We'd only been married for two years when he had decided to go to Afghanistan, and I had just graduated from graduate school. It seemed like we were just getting started, and I couldn't wait to see what the future would bring. Nothing, absolutely nothing, could have prepared me for what happened next. My cloud nine was about to disintegrate into a million pieces. My upcoming weekly call with my husband would change everything.

Scott called at his usual time. We talked about our day, and I filled him in on everything I was doing around the house. I had painted several rooms and had begun decorating some of them. I told him about my plans for each room and asked for his opinion on all of my ideas. Our conversation was light and loving, just like always. As our talk started to wind down, my husband dropped a bombshell.

"I'm thinking about signing up for another year," he said. I was stunned, and believe me, there was dead silence. I couldn't believe what I had just heard. Tears began welling up in my eyes and I felt like my heart had just been ripped apart. *How could he not want to be with me?* is all that came into my head. I choked back the tears and started asking why he wanted to do such a thing. It really didn't matter what he said, because all I heard was, *I don't love you enough to come home.* Yep, that was my sick ego telling me lies. And I believed them. I was angry and hurt all over again, but this time felt so much worse. Once again,

I refused to tell Scott my true feelings, but this time was different. I wasn't holding back out of fear of hurting him. I was pissed off, and I was just going to wallow in my own ugly feelings. Somehow, I guess I thought that he would notice and just decide to come home, but all it ended up doing, as you will see, was to lead me to a place of victimhood, self-sabotage, illness, and lots of other bad stuff.

I had felt restless for several months, and after hearing that my husband wanted to sign up for another year, I knew I had to do something. I couldn't imagine going another year without Scott by my side. I felt more lost than I had before, and I was ready to make some changes. *I'm not just going to sit here and wait until he's ready to come home,* I told myself. But what was I going to do? I began calling on the angels for help and would often cry out in desperation.

"Please, angels, show me what to do. Show me where to go. I need your help." As I prayed to the angels for guidance, the pull to Pennsylvania grew stronger and stronger. I didn't know why. Maybe I just needed a new start. Maybe I was running from something, or maybe I was running *to* something. I didn't really know what was going on, but I knew that my life was not where I thought it would be. "I didn't sign up for this!" I would often scream. What had happened to my perfect life? After things had sunk in for a few days, I decided to take a trip to Pennsylvania once again. Maybe another trip to those beautiful mountains would give me some sort of insight. All I knew is that I always felt better after being there, so I booked another ticket and headed to the Poconos the following month.

My trip was amazing. I saw so many friends and had a wonderful time. I drove around the nearby towns and looked at properties at a nearby lake. My trip had shifted from "just visiting" to looking for somewhere to live. I felt myself longing to be there in those mountains and didn't want to leave. I didn't know it at the time, but everything was being orchestrated for me. There were things going on "behind the scenes" that I wasn't aware of. My guides and angels were steering me forward toward my destiny without me even knowing it. I was being called to those mountains, where I would be tested beyond my wildest expectations. The Endless Mountains of Pennsylvania would prove to be sacred ground for me. They would hold so many of my tears, breakthroughs, defeats, and triumphs. Those mountains would help me get to the other side: the other side of grief, disgust, guilt, self-loathing, disease, and even rock bottom. Those mountains would prove to be the catalyst to my true awakening.

Chapter 4

A New Start

When I returned to my home in Kansas, I decided it was time for a change. During our next phone call, I told Scott that I wanted to move to Pennsylvania. I remember saying something real stupid and sarcastic, like, "Well, if you can decide to go to Afghanistan and stay another year, then I can make this decision on my own too." I know, it sounds like all kinds of crazy, but remember, my ego was running the show, telling me lies and making me believe all kinds of crap. I was still hurt and angry and wanted desperately to fix the pain inside. Somehow, I just knew that moving to Pennsylvania was the next step for me. I put our house on the market, began packing all of our things, and secured a place to live. In no time, I was on my way to those Endless Mountains, where my life would take so many twists and turns. I had no idea of all of the amazing (and sometimes not-so-amazing) things that were waiting to reveal themselves to me. This, my friend, was where life began to get interesting!

As I settled into my new home in Pennsylvania, I continued my career as a speech-language pathologist, working with elderly clients as well as young children. I decided to open a private practice, as I had been successful at building one in Kansas. I lived in a small home in the woods, close to one of the area's largest lakes. Although I had neighbors, they were seasonal and not around often. It made for the perfect little secluded spot where I could spend time in solitude and even crank my music up and dance when I felt like it. I just loved my little house, although it needed so many updates. A little old couple, both of who had passed away, had owned it before we did. My husband and I had purchased the home with all of its contents, as the family just wanted to sell it quickly after their passing. There was so much stuff, and I would imagine their life together as I sifted through the contents. I just adored my new home and felt so peaceful when I was there. I couldn't wait to return home after work each afternoon and take walks outside with my dog and swing in my hammock. I spent my time reading, listening to beautiful music, and watching the deer play in my yard. My little red house would prove to be so much more than just a place to put up my feet and rest. It would serve as a place of incredible self-realization.

My life took so many twists and turns over the next several years. My marriage, once such a magical union, would not withstand the test of time. The pain inside had grown too much to bear, and I sought love in someone else's arms. I had an affair. And if the pain I already felt from missing my soul mate wasn't enough, it only grew worse when I decided to commit the ultimate betrayal. And although I had turned towards one of the kindest and sweetest men I had ever met, my internal struggle grew deeper. I had such disgust, guilt, and shame for what I was doing, which only grew deeper day by day. Let me just say one thing here. If you have issues with loving yourself, as I did, having an affair will really fuck things up. I'm not passing judgment. Believe me. I'm just telling it like it is in the hopes that it might spare some of you the horrible self-loathing that can accompany such an act. It took me several years to finally forgive myself for what I had done, and I don't wish that on anyone. In hindsight I can say that I learned one of the most important, and most difficult, lessons of my life. You cannot fill what is missing within yourself with anyone else. You must learn to love yourself first.

Needless to say, my marriage did not survive. As time went on, the bond that we had once shared completely disintegrated. I know that neither one of us meant to hurt the other, but so much hurt had occurred. Too much to mend, I guess. As discussions of divorce began to take the forefront, I knew that both of our hearts were breaking into pieces. I called on the angels to help us both—to help us heal, whatever that meant for each of us. I asked them to help me forgive myself for not being the wife that I wished I could've been. I asked them to be with Scott and help him heal from the whole ordeal. I knew we both felt lost, but I knew deep in my heart that the angels would be able to help. Our journey together came to an end and we were each forced to find a different path, a path that would lead us to the next chapter in our lives.

As time moved on, I slowly began to heal. The resentment and anger that I had for myself had a strong hold, but I continued to work with the angels daily to let it go. My heart ached for what I had once had, and I would cry out in desperation. "I just can't go on like this! Please, angels, help me let go of the pain." I worked with Archangel Michael frequently, cutting cords to the past so that I could try to heal. I struggled with self-forgiveness and self-worth and had to begin using daily mantras, just to convince myself I was worth a damn. Although I felt alone in the physical sense, I knew the angels were constantly around me. I could feel them surround me as soon as I called on them, and if I closed my eyes, I could even see them. I had "healing sessions" with them every evening where I would lie down and envision my body. I would often see so many holes where I held lower vibrational emotions like sadness, guilt, and shame. I would lie there and ask the angels to fill me up and to make me whole again. I felt their presence around me and knew that they were doing their best. It was my own struggle with forgiving myself that was getting in the way. The angels had the ability to heal me completely if I would just surrender. All I needed to do was to forgive myself and let go.

Life continued and, gradually, so did my healing. With each day, I began to feel a little better. I started to let go of the past and realized that there was nothing that I could do to change it now. My only choice was to move forward and try to do things better. I knew I had to forgive myself and continued to ask the angels to help me do just that. I continued to pray and meditate daily, and over time, I began to feel my heart getting full again. During meditation, I would often envision my heart being infused with love and light. Over time, it began to glow brighter and brighter as I released all of the crap that wasn't serving me anymore. The angels were answering my prayers. They were filling me up. They were helping me heal so that I could find love again.

My life was pretty simple and peaceful. I worked during the day as a speech pathologist, helping my clients improve their lives in any way I could. I never worked alone, as I called the angels in to help me with each and every client. When meeting new clients, I would always ask them what their ideal outcome looked like. I guess I knew intuitively of the importance of clients voicing their desires and sending it out to the universe. I can't begin to tell you the number of miracles I witnessed. And I believe they were primarily due to the fact that my clients not only sent their hopes, prayers, and expectations to God and the angels, but that they expected to receive what they had asked for. After hearing my many clients' wishes, I would always add something like, "Well, let's call on the angels and ask them to help you with this." I remember one gentleman in particular who made what most in the medical field would consider a miraculous recovery.

I met a sweet, older gentleman while working for one of the area's long-term care/rehab facilities. Jim had arrived at the facility after suffering a very serious and debilitating stroke. I visited with Jim and his wife during his initial evaluation. He had very slurred speech that was quite difficult to understand, and his swallowing mechanism was compromised. Jim had to be placed on a soft diet, as he was at risk for silent aspiration. Although I don't recall all of the details from the doctor's report, I do remember that Jim's prognosis was grim. The doctor didn't feel that there was much hope for Jim to be able to return to a regular diet, as he felt the damage that had been done was permanent. As I completed Jim's evaluation to determine the best course of action, I asked him what he wanted his outcome to be.

"What would you like to be able to do?" I asked him. Although some of Jim's responses were a bit difficult to understand, he was very clear in what he wanted to be able to eat in the future.

"I want steak," he announced, loud and clear.

"Well, let's get the angels on it, and you and I will get to work. I believe in miracles, Jim, and I'm sure there is one waiting for you. I can't wait to see you eat a steak again," I replied.

Jim's determination was inspirational. He did everything I asked him to and would even ask for extra "homework." We worked together for several months, and Jim began to make amazing progress. I would call the angels in before every session and ask them to "bring on the miracles." With a little help from the angels, Jim's drive and determination finally paid off. Miraculously, his speech and swallowing abilities returned to normal. They didn't just get better. They were normal. It was finally time for Jim to leave and go back home. He and his wife stopped by my office to say good-bye. I gave Jim a big hug and told him I was blessed to have known him.

"You've taught me so much," I said. "You are amazing."

Jim grinned from ear to ear as he listened to my words. He thanked me for helping him get back to his "old self" and then said, "My wife's making me a steak tonight."

We both began laughing, and the joy that filled that room was priceless! Jim had asked for what he wanted, put in the hard work, and never wavered in his faith that he would eat steak again someday, and the angels had brought on his miracle. I thanked the angels for helping Jim and for allowing me to see this miracle unfold.

"This shit is amazing," I said under my breath. "I'm ready for more."

My new life was beginning in the Endless Mountains of Pennsylvania. I worked during the day seeing clients of all ages. In the evening, I would spend time reading spiritual books, walking in the woods around my house, meditating, and listening to uplifting music. I rarely watched television, as I rarely found anything worth watching. I used my angel oracle cards daily and would meditate with the angels often. As my connection with the angels grew even stronger, I felt myself becoming more and more sensitive to the energies around me. It became difficult to be around negativity of any kind: people, television, and the like. I spent many hours doing walking meditations outside in nature. I felt so connected to God and the angels when I walked among the trees. Walking in nature helped me heal from the pain I still carried from my failed marriage. Being in nature had a calming effect on me, and I couldn't wait to get home each day from work and walk with my dogs. The more I walked, the more "in tune" I became.

Before long, I was able to hear God and the angels. Not like hearing voices when you're speaking with someone; I heard them in my head. Their messages were so loving and supportive, always letting me know that I wasn't alone.

I would begin my walks sometimes by asking particular questions and at other times, just by asking things like "What do you want me to know?" I began to get visions and ideas and knew that my connection was growing. As I forgave myself for things I had done in the past, I began to hear more clearly. Whatever was happening was a beautiful thing. I felt myself shifting into a new space, one of love, hope, and compassion. I would smile as I walked each day, and it wasn't long before I began noticing all of the little miracles that had been right in front of me all along. Butterflies and dragonflies began to accompany me on my walks. Not in large numbers or anything, but it was common to have one or the other fly along with me as I walked. As I continued my daily walks with God and the angels, I found myself in a place of gratitude. I thanked them for all of the wonderful things I got to see each day. And I began to notice that the more gratitude I gave, the more amazing things I saw.

As my connection with God and the angels increased, so did my awareness. I began to look at things differently. I started noticing things around me that I had not really tuned into before. There was such beauty all around me, and I began to take notice. I remembered having that sense of wonder as a child, but it had gotten lost somewhere in the shuffle of life. That inner child was being reawakened, and I was beginning to see the world from unclouded lenses once again. I would often thank God for opening my eyes to all that I had taken for granted. Oh, how I had gotten lost somewhere along the way! That dark and lonely place that I had found myself in was becoming a thing of the past. I saw light on the horizon. My glass became half full. I knew that I was being led. Led out of darkness and despair and toward something so much more. I didn't know what it was at the time, but many refer to it as destiny. I called out to God and the angels and told them to lead the way.

"I will follow wherever you want me to go," I said. "Just tell me what to do and I will do it." I said it and I meant it. I felt the love that God and the angels had for me, and I never wanted it to end.

Chapter 5

The Woman in the Window

As I continued on my spiritual journey, I became more and more sensitive to everything around me. It was crazy how things in my physical body began to shift as the emotional and spiritual part of me came into alignment. My abilities to feel, hear, know, and just sense things increased, and I knew that my level of awareness was beginning to reach heights that I had never experienced before. One evening, as I was washing dishes, I glanced out of the window that hung above the sink, as I had done many times before. I would often catch a glimpse of deer playing in my yard, often several at a time. The doe would bring their young fawns to frolic in my yard, and they always put on quite a show. This particular evening, it was dark out, and the deer had turned in for the night. It was dark enough that I couldn't see outside—only my own reflection in the window glass. I continued washing dishes as I listened to music, singing along to the familiar songs.

As I sang, I glanced up at the window from time to time. I'm sure you can imagine my surprise when, during one of those glances in the window, I noticed someone else looking back at me. I saw myself in the window, but suddenly, there was an older woman standing directly behind me, looking right at me. Our eyes locked and she began to smile. The look in her eyes was so loving, and I felt so much kindness and compassion coming from her. I didn't recognize her, but she somehow felt so familiar. Although this was absolutely nothing I had ever experienced before, I wasn't scared at all. I couldn't get over how loving she felt as she smiled at me, and I felt as if she was there to help me. It was as if she was letting me know that everything was going to be all right. I looked down to rinse the dish I was holding and quickly gazed back at the window. She was gone. She had disappeared just as quickly as she had appeared. I looked away and back into the window several times, trying to get a glimpse of her again, but she never came. *Who was she?* I wondered. *Was she the owner of the house? Was she keeping an eye on the place?* I had so many questions running through my mind. As I had done so many times before, I asked the angels for guidance.

"Who is that woman?" I asked them as I laid my head down to sleep that evening. I would often ask questions before going to bed, as that seemed to be a time I received lots of answers. I left it in the angel's hands and drifted off to sleep.

I woke the next day with the strong feeling that the little old woman I had seen the night before was indeed the owner of my home. I wasn't sure why she was still there, but I didn't feel threatened or nervous in any way with the notion that she was hanging around. I actually felt comfort in knowing that she was there. Perhaps she was helping me behind the scenes somehow. Perhaps she was acting as one of my guardian angels. Whatever the case, I knew I felt better having her around. Her sweet and gentle spirit seemed to put me at ease somehow. I welcomed her presence and any guidance she might be able to lend me.

I saw the woman's reflection a handful of times over the next few years. She never said anything, only smiled ever so sweetly at me. She would appear at times when I was feeling sad or lonely, and I knew she was letting me know that she was sending love. I felt such a reassuring feeling coming from her, a feeling that everything was going to be okay. I felt that she had shown up as one of my guides, to offer love and support. We never spoke. Our exchanges were only simple smiles of love and gratitude. And even though there were no words ever spoken between us, it would prove to be one of the most amazing exchanges of love that I would ever feel.

Chapter 6

Hitting Rock Bottom

I mentioned earlier in my book that the Endless Mountains of Pennsylvania were witness to many of my trials and tribulations. Although so many wonderful things were happening within and around me, something not so wonderful was beginning to fester inside of me. My health began to take a turn, and I was in unfamiliar territory. I had always been an active person and even worked out with a personal trainer three times per week. I began to notice things happening with my body that were far from desirable. My joints ached, and I often suffered from migraines and neck pain and stiffness. My workouts became too painful to take and I had to finally stop them altogether. In no time at all, my list of symptoms was growing longer and longer. I experienced dizziness and vertigo daily, and my hands would shake from time to time. Confusion and mood swings were frequent, and I began to ride some sort of crazy, emotional roller coaster. My feeling of "connectedness" seemed to be fading, and I soon found myself on an inhaler for breathing difficulties and medication for panic attacks. I had no idea what was happening to me, but I knew it was bad, and I needed help.

I visited specialist after specialist in search of answers to my growing list of ailments. One recommended that I get a breast reduction to ease my neck pain. I laughed at him and asked, "But what about the other forty symptoms I described?"

The next doctor suggested I take a round of what I consider to be very dangerous drugs. "It'll help me make a diagnosis," he told me.

My answer was plain and simple. "If you can't tell me what's wrong with me, I'm sure as heck not going to take those drugs with the hope that you figure it out."

The last doctor I saw topped the rest. After doing more blood work—the same blood work I had had done every other time—he said that he could find nothing wrong with me. See, that's the problem. My blood work would come back perfect, but I was falling apart. That last doctor came into my room and said, "I think this is all in your head, and I think you need to see a psychiatrist."

Let me tell you, I was beyond frustrated at this point. And yes, I was going to need a psychiatrist because I literally thought I was going to kill someone. I knew something was going on inside of my body, but no one could figure out what it was. And now this doctor didn't even believe me. I left his office feeling beaten down and defeated. I had nowhere else to turn, and I found myself spiraling quickly toward a very dark place.

As my health declined even further, I found it increasingly difficult to function most days. Since I wasn't getting any help from the medical community, I began looking into alternative healing methods. I started seeing a Reiki practitioner and received weekly treatments. I purchased CDs that were filled with positive affirmations and listened to them daily. Although I'd had to give up working out with my trainer, I continued walking, as I knew I had to keep moving, no matter what. I feared what would happen if I let myself stop completely. Giving up meant death to me, and that just wasn't an option. I listened to my CDs as I walked and repeated things like, "I am strong. I am healthy. I am whole," even as my beaten-down body told me otherwise. Fatigue, hopelessness, and a broken spirit were beginning to take hold, and there seemed to be nothing I could do about it. I was eventually forced to close my private practice because it just became too difficult to make it to my office and keep it running. I kept my contracting jobs, which at least brought in some income. The closing of my office brought with it its own emotional roller coaster. My practice had been booming just months before, and now I was forced to close my doors. My dreams were dashed, and I felt like a complete failure. *How could this have happened to me?* I wondered. Was this some sort of punishment for all of the things I had done? The voice was strong in my head, trying to convince me that I deserved all of this. And if you don't already know for yourself, victimhood is no place you want to be. As I tried desperately to keep my head above water, I continued calling in the angels. I tried not to allow negative thoughts in my head, but it was growing increasingly difficult to keep them away. My angels weren't answering me, and I didn't understand why.

Chapter 7

Pilgrimage to Sedona

My life was definitely not what I had envisioned it to be. I was going through a devastating divorce, I had a debilitating illness that no one could diagnose, I had to close my private practice, I had very few friends, and my family was halfway across the country. I felt completely isolated and alone. I cried a lot and begged the angels to help me. I even changed what I asked for, in case it would mean I would receive answers. Instead of asking for miraculous healing, I now found myself asking for them to bring me anyone who could help me. "Please, angels, bring helpful people to me, anyone who can help me out of this hole I've ended up in." Amazingly, as soon as I changed my prayers from "please heal me" to "please help me heal myself," the angels delivered my message.

One of the friends I had made in Pennsylvania told me about an upcoming retreat she had heard about. A woman she knew was hosting a "pilgrimage to Sedona." I don't recall ever hearing about Sedona before this particular conversation, but as soon as I heard that it was a pilgrimage, I just knew I was supposed to go. Something seemed to light up inside me as I read details about the trip. This was what I needed. This trip was going to change my life, and I knew I had to get there. But how was I going to come up with all of that money? The trip cost $963, which was way more than I had at the time. I hadn't worked much in the past few months, and I was sinking deeply in debt. My health had deteriorated and I could hardly manage to crawl out of bed some days. I barely had a penny to my name, and my body was falling apart. But, for some reason, I just knew Sedona held the answers. I called on the angels and made my request plain and simple. "Angels, if I'm supposed to go on this trip to Sedona, please bring me the money. I know you have resources that I could never dream about, so I am leaving it in your hands." That was it. I left it with the angels and I let it go.

About two weeks later, I ran down to check the mail. I lived in a lake community and everyone's mailboxes were in a central location near the clubhouse, about a mile from my home. I had a stack of bills, as usual, which I tossed to the side for later. It was agony to open my bills, as I knew I was getting farther and farther behind in paying them. Halfway through sorting, I noticed a letter from my insurance company. I wondered what it could be, since I had already sent my payment in to them. I opened the letter and pulled the contents out. I couldn't believe my eyes! There, in my hand, was a check for exactly $963. No kidding! I unfolded the letter and read frantically. According to my insurance company, it was some sort of refund. I had overpaid or something. To be honest, I don't remember the exact wording of the letter, just that it was a refund of some sort. I began jumping up and down, thanking the angels. I laughed and danced around as if I had won the lottery. I was thrilled, and I was grateful. I contacted the woman who was hosting the trip to Sedona and secured a spot for the pilgrimage. I knew the angels had arranged everything, and I knew something big was going to happen.

The time came for our pilgrimage to begin. A small group of us landed in Phoenix, where a shuttle was scheduled to pick us up and take us to our final destination. There were about forty of us who had traveled from all over the world, and most of us had had a long day, touching down at various airports before finally landing in Phoenix. Some of us had contacted each other before the trip and planned to meet in the baggage claim area. Most of us had never met before, but we felt an instant connection when we laid eyes on each other. We felt like family. We hugged each other as if we had known each other forever. Once everyone was accounted for, we made our way outside, where we were greeted by our shuttle driver. Paul was going to be taking us on the final leg of our journey to Sedona. Sedona lies about ninety minutes north of Phoenix and is home to some of the most amazing red-rock formations I have ever seen. It's also home to a number of vortexes that you just have to experience for yourself.

Paul was a jolly, older fellow. He was full of stories and jokes and kept us laughing the entire trip. Many of us began to share stories about how we had heard about this pilgrimage and how each of us felt drawn to be a part of it. Although everyone had a different reason for being there, we all felt some sort of kinship. We knew that we were supposed to be on this journey together, and we couldn't wait to see what the week would bring. I'm certain none of us felt the magnitude of what was going to happen. It would prove to be one of the most amazing and life-changing weeks of our lives.

As our bus pulled into our new home for the next week, we all breathed a sigh of relief. Many of us had traveled so far and were ready to have our feet on the ground. The door of the bus opened, and as we stepped out onto the red ground, we felt such a calmness come over us. We had arrived at something amazing, and we could feel the love that surrounded us. We gathered our things and walked toward the main building to check in. As we got close to the entryway, we noticed so many hummingbirds. They were everywhere! They flew all around us, and we all watched in amazement. It was as if they were the welcoming committee, coming to say hello. We giggled like little children as they buzzed around our heads.

The staff was so kind, helpful, and loving and seemed so glad to see us, as if they'd been waiting a lifetime for our arrival. They greeted us with hugs and welcomed us into their space. I was already beginning to get filled up with so much love and the retreat hadn't even started. "Thank you, angels. Thank you. Thank you," I kept saying under my breath. I knew that I was in a magical place, and I was grateful for the opportunities that lay ahead of me.

After everyone had gotten checked in, my small group of six made our way to our bungalow, where we would be staying for the week. It was a beautiful little orange house with several bedrooms, a living room, and a kitchen. I made my way to the room to which I had been assigned, and hanging right above the door was a plaque. Each bedroom had a plaque with a unique name engraved on it. Mine read, "The Hawk Room." I had no idea at the time that this was actually one of my spirit animal guides making an introduction. My hawk would continue as one of my spirit guides from that day on.

We all gathered for a group introduction that evening. We were weathered and worn but so excited to be together. We sat in a circle, all forty of us, and introduced ourselves to the group. We were asked to share our names, where we were from, and why we were there. As others in the group shared their stories, my heart began to race. *Why am I here?* I wondered. I knew that I wanted to learn more about the angels and the afterlife, but I also knew there was a much bigger reason I was sitting in this circle of strangers. As people continued to share their stories, the time had come for me to share mine. I didn't know what I was going to say. I closed my eyes and just began to speak.

"My name's Julia, and I'm from Pennsylvania." I paused for a moment, and before I knew it, the words just came spilling out of my mouth. "I'm here because I'm broken." Tears started pouring down my cheeks and I began sobbing. Until that very moment, I don't think I had realized how truly broken I felt. So many emotions began to come to the surface in those few silent moments. I noticed as other people in the circle began wiping tears from their eyes. Many were nodding their heads as if they understood. The leader of our group spoke up and thanked me for digging deep and being honest.

"There's probably several of you that can relate to Julia," she said. Several group members nodded their heads again, saying yes. As I gained my composure, I felt like I had just released such a burden. Just saying those words, "I'm broken," seemed to release so much that was pent-up inside of me. I couldn't believe how much lighter I felt. I felt surrounded by so many angels and felt completely loved at that moment. I knew that I was there to heal, and I knew that things would never be the same.

The next day, I woke feeling rested and rejuvenated. I made my way to breakfast, where I met with the rest of our group. The menu was organic, vegetarian, and simply amazing. There was an abundance of freshly made pastries, grains, eggs, vegetables, and fruits. My body smiled as I filled it up with so many healing foods. The group sat together, talking and laughing about what had happened the night before. I can honestly say that everyone looked completely different. I mean, it was crazy how everyone's energy had shifted in such a short time. Everyone looked brighter and younger, and everyone was glowing. I can only imagine that it had so much to do with what we had tapped into and released the night before. It was apparent that we all had been carrying so many burdens, and the weight of them had literally affected our outward appearances.

After breakfast, we all met in one of the larger buildings. It was a beautiful room surrounded with windows that reached from floor to ceiling. The sun was shining in, and we enjoyed watching all of the animals playing outside. There were birds, squirrels, and rabbits playing outside and several butterflies and dragonflies flying about. We sat in a circle and began sharing our experiences of how we were led to be a part of this pilgrimage. Everyone had very different and interesting stories, but it seemed that we all had a common goal: to gain a stronger connection with the realms above and open up to all of the possibilities that lay ahead for each and every one of us. Most of us expressed a burning desire to help others and felt that we were here to do big things. Our leader guided us into meditation, where we were able to connect and receive love and guidance. I'm not sure that I received a whole lot of guidance that first time, but I felt completely at peace, something I truly hadn't ever felt before—at least, not on this level. My mind, body, and spirit were completely still, and it was the first time I was able to just be.

One of the first exercises we were asked to participate in was to spend a few hours in silence. We were to be completely silent and to spend time alone until our evening meal. Most of us had never done this before, and we giggled at the thought of not talking to anyone for several hours. This simple exercise would prove to be yet another turning point in my life. I'll have to admit, it seemed a bit strange at first. No one talked or really even looked at each other as we passed each other on the various trails. It's amazing how much beauty one can notice when spending time in silence. I began to notice so many birds and butterflies. I would sit in silence near the stream behind our little, orange house and noticed the water flowing over the rocks on a whole new level. It sounded different. Louder. It was a cleansing sound, and I envisioned it cleansing my body of any impurities. I walked and walked for what seemed like hours, and I didn't want to stop. The more I walked, the better I felt. The birds singing nearby seemed louder than I had noticed before. I began to notice all sorts of little animals scurrying around me wherever I sat. They weren't scared and seemed more curious than anything. There were bunnies and squirrels playing about and even a hummingbird that would stop by to visit me several times that day, hovering right in front of my face as if it was trying to tell me something. It was magical, and I found myself engulfed in a state of wonder as I continued my walking meditation. It wasn't long before my inner child, that child inside that had been forgotten about for so long ago, began to come to the surface again. That dear, sweet, innocent child who knew that anything and everything was possible came peeking out once again, and I was so happy to welcome her back.

As I walked in silence, noticing all of the beauty around me, I began to feel closer to God. I walked along the trails and hiked some of the hills, taking in all of the magnificence that God had created. I asked God to walk with me and asked Him to give me guidance. I felt so loved as I continued and felt that He was walking right beside me. "Let me see things through your eyes," I prayed, which is something I say even to this day. I began to notice even more butterflies and their intricate colors. I noticed several small angel statues that hadn't caught my eye before and felt the love coming from each of them. It felt as if they were manning their post and keeping a watch on everything, ensuring that everyone felt loved. I noticed the flowers and really began to see their different colors pop. It was as if they all had different personalities, which came through in their individual and unique colors. I passed by some ferns whose branches appeared to be waving in the wind; however, there wasn't a breeze of any kind. "They are waving at me," I said to myself. It was as if they were cheering me on. *This is how God sees things*, I thought to myself. *He sees the beauty in everything.*

I began to notice a bird following me as I walked. He was a small bird with a white breast and black head. I thanked him for appearing to me and thanked him for his beautiful voice, as he would chirp in my direction from time to time. After I first noticed him, that little bird continued to follow me for the rest of the afternoon. He was everywhere. He would show up perched in various trees as I hiked the different trails and surrounding hills. He was even waiting on the banister outside of my cabin when I stopped to freshen up. That little bird followed me all day, sharing his beautiful voice with me, and he was always looking right at me while he chirped. Suddenly, something dawned on me. Maybe this little bird was trying to tell me something. Maybe he had a message for me. I had heard about people who were able to communicate with animals, but I would've never thought that I would be one of them. I stopped dead in my tracks and looked at the bird, which had just landed in a tree over my left shoulder. He just sat there and looked at me, tilting his little head back and forth. Although it was probably only seconds, it felt like we had stared at each other for several minutes. I finally asked the little bird, "What are you trying to tell me?" As soon as I had uttered those words, that little bird turned around. He had his back to me now and sat so still. He turned his head and looked back at me as if to say, "Here's your message." I was instantly drawn to a big *V* on his back. It was black and quite noticeable, as his body was white and light brown in color. As I noticed this *V,* I instantly heard, *Victory!* It was something I heard in my head, but it was as loud as if someone had shouted it at me. Tears began to roll down my face. This was my answer. I knew that God was assuring me that everything was going to be okay. I was headed toward victory, even if I didn't know how I would get there. The amount of love and support I felt at that very moment is hard to put into words. It was as if heaven had come swooping down and embraced me with all its might. I knew that God had heard my prayers and I knew that my miracle was on its way.

The week was filled with so many magical things. The red rocks of Sedona had very graciously eased me of my burdens. I had released so much that had weighed me down for so long, and I was ready to learn to love myself again. I had forgiven those who had hurt me, and, more importantly, I had forgiven myself. I was ready to start a new chapter in my life, one filled with love and compassion. I was hopeful about the future and could see a light at the end of the tunnel now. My healing had begun and I was ready for whatever lay ahead of me. I said good-bye to my new friends and gathered my things for my flight home. I had left Pennsylvania so broken, but I was returning with a renewed spirit. I made a decision right then and there that I would never let myself go to that dark place ever again.

Chapter 8

Meeting My Spirit Guide

I returned to Pennsylvania feeling unstoppable. I wanted to learn as much as I could about communicating with animals, now that I knew I was able to do it. I purchased a book that taught about animal spirit guides and the various messages that each animal brings with it. I was fascinated to learn of all of their different messages and was eager to receive some of my own. In no time, they began speaking to me. I started seeing so many animals around my home—so many more than I'd ever seen before. At times, I would just know what they were there to tell me, and at others, I would reference my book. Their messages always made sense and came at times that I needed them most. Over the years, I was able to fine-tune my ability to connect with animals and have enjoyed communicating with them for many of my clients and for myself.

So, now I was able to communicate with angels and animals. *Hmm,* I thought, *what's next?* I continued my quest in being able to connect with the realms above and read just about anything I could get my hands on. I began to learn about spirit guides and how each of us may have one or several who have been assigned to help us on our journey. I learned how these guides help us fulfill our assignments here on earth and guide us toward our destiny. We may have highly ascended masters, such as Jesus or Buddha, offering help throughout our lifetime, as well as several other guides who come in and out of our lives when we need specific help from them. Some of our guides may be working only with us, while others may work with many people during the same lifetime. I learned that our spirit guides reveal themselves to us when we're ready, often when we are in need of their wisdom and guidance. So, I began talking to my guides, telling them that I was ready to meet them whenever they felt it was time. I guess I was ready, as just a few weeks later, I would connect with a very brave and wise soul.

As time went on, I began to feel an even deeper connection with God and the angels. I would walk daily, in meditation, and feel such a sense of peace. My eyes began to open up to all of the amazing things around me. I gained a stronger connection with the earth, the trees, plants, and the animals that lived in the forest around my house. I began to see visions while meditating that were becoming clearer and clearer, and so much was shifting inside of me. I practiced many forms of meditation, such as guided meditations, silent meditations, and walking meditations, as I enjoyed a variety of things. It was during one of these meditations that I would meet one of my spirit guides for the very first time.

I purchased a meditation online that was called "Reiki Psychic Attunement." I had been attuned to Reiki levels one and two but felt drawn to this particular meditation for some reason. I recall stumbling across it while surfing the Internet one day and knew it was something I needed to get. I received my DVD and couldn't wait to watch it. The guide for the Reiki attunement demonstrated a number of hand movements that I was supposed to do during the attunement. I was to do these movements while staring at a large, clear quartz crystal that was placed on a rock at the Bell Rock vortex in Sedona, Arizona. It amazed me that Sedona was still playing a part of my healing and transformation, even from thousands of miles away.

The meditation began and I followed the instructor's guidance as he told me where to place my hands. I could feel the energy increasing inside of my body with each hand position and even began to see colors. The energy around my eyes and forehead seemed to be shifting as I stared at the crystal in front of me. I began to see what appeared to be some sort of film being removed from my eyes. I know it sounds crazy, but that's what started happening. It wasn't painful or uncomfortable, and I felt like someone or something was helping me to be able to see clearer, both with my physical eyes as well as with my "third eye." When the attunement was complete, I was instructed to sit quietly and stare at the clear quartz crystal for several minutes. By this time, I was completely relaxed and my body felt so heavy that I could barely move. I stared at the crystal for what felt like a very long time. Nothing happened at first, but as my gaze softened and I stopped trying so hard to see something, things began to shift. I began to see images within the crystal. They began shifting into different shapes that would remain still for different periods of time. The first image I saw was that of wolf's face. It was staring right at me, and I got a sense of protection. That was the word that came to mind: *protected,* and I felt it was a message for me letting me know that he was protecting me. The wolf seemed to stare at me, as if we had known each other for eternity. The wolf came with messages of love and courage, letting me know that I was fully supported. Like the little woman in the window, there were no words spoken—just a "knowing" of what my message was. I thanked the wolf for his messages as tears began to well up in my eyes. I felt so connected to him and knew that we had somehow traveled together before.

The wolf's face appeared for several minutes and then began to shift into something else. As the picture changed, two faces began to come into focus. They were men's faces and seemed so familiar to me. The men looked weathered and worn, and I felt such wisdom coming from their weary eyes. I knew that they were Native American. Possibly chiefs. One of them wore a beautiful headdress. They looked as they had so much to tell me, if only I could hear what they had to say. I stared at the two faces for the remainder of the meditation. When it was over, and the instructor began to speak again, the two faces slowly disappeared. *Who were these men?* I wondered. *And what do they want with me?*

When the meditation had ended, I sat quietly, taking in everything that had just occurred. I had never experienced anything like that and certainly hadn't had any visions before. I felt that some sort of channel had just been opened or something. Something had happened during that meditation, perhaps when that film was being removed from my eyes. I was understandably a little shocked and amazed at what had occurred. I felt such a strong connection to these men, especially the one wearing a headdress. I had a feeling he was my spirit guide, and I was eager to find out who he was.

That evening, I decided to get online to see if I could find either of the men that I had seen during the meditation. I typed "Native American Chiefs" into the search engine and began to scour over hundreds and hundreds of pictures. I'm not sure how long I searched online that night, but it seemed like hours. It was getting late and I was growing tired, but I wanted desperately to find out who these men were. I knew deep down that it was important for me to find out who they were, as I just knew they had come to me for a reason. I was just about ready to give up my search when, low and behold, I found one of them. I found a picture of one of the men that looked exactly like the picture I had seen in the crystal. It was a picture of the man wearing the headdress. I clicked on the photo and read the description: "Chief Joseph of the Nez Perce Tribe." I was completely blown away. I couldn't believe that I had found the exact picture that I had seen earlier that day in meditation. I sat there for a few minutes just staring at the photo. Tears came to my eyes as I began to feel a deep, unexplainable connection to the man on my screen. It was some sort of "soul link" or something—really nothing I can put into words. I felt his courage and strength but also a deep sense of loss and sadness. I knew that he had seen so much and lost so much during his lifetime and I could feel his pain. I didn't know why he had chosen me, but I knew that Chief Joseph was stepping forward to help me for some reason. I knew that he was stepping forward as one of my guides, and I welcomed any guidance and wisdom he had come to offer me.

My connection with Chief Joseph just felt so right. Over time, I was able to find pictures of the chief, which I displayed throughout my home. About a week after my initial encounter with the chief, I connected with him once again. I had made an appointment with a homeopath in my area. I continued to struggle with several physical issues and had heard about someone through word of mouth. As I walked into the homeopath's waiting room, there stood a large picture of Chief Joseph with a poem inscribed beside it. I knew it was a message for me, that I was headed in the right direction. I told the woman what had happened the week before, how I had connected with the chief through a guided meditation. She just giggled and replied, "I think Chief Joseph is bringing lots of us together."

I felt at ease, knowing that Chief Joseph was guiding me to those who might be able to help me, and I thanked him for being by my side. I didn't get all of the answers about my health condition that day, but I did get some help. I started a regime of natural supplements, which started me down my path of regaining my health. I'll talk more a bit later about how I ended up finally getting a correct diagnosis. For now, it's all about Chief Joseph.

I remained connected with Chief Joseph for the next few years. I felt quite close to him and would often picture his tribe drumming over the land around my home. I felt they were drumming not only to help heal Mother Earth, but to help me on my journey as well. I felt a strong sense that they were drumming to fill me with courage and strength, and I could feel so many amazingly strong beings standing by my side. My tribe was guiding me on my way.

Over a period of time, I seemed to drift away from Chief Joseph. Maybe it was true what some of the books had said. Maybe our spirit guides come in and out of our lives, as we need them to. Maybe he stepped back so others could guide me. Whatever the case may be, I reconnected with him once again. That "reconnection" happened while writing this book, and I was guided to include the story of how it happened so that you might see that our guides do, in fact, come into our lives when we need them. They will show up and let you know they are near when it's time for them to guide you once again. Just be open to how they might connect with you and they will find a way to do so. I think you will agree, after reading my next story, that Chief Joseph was definitely letting me know that he was there to guide me once again.

I had taken some time off to rest, get filled up, and write. I did this periodically when I would begin to feel drained or when I just needed to take a break. I had rented a beautiful little house in Massachusetts where I would spend a blessed two months with my two little dogs, Daisy and Rosie. I enjoyed my time there and focused on getting lots of rest, doing yoga, meditating, walking in a nearby park, and taking drives along the countryside. I would often load up my dogs and take long drives along the many beautiful country roads. The scenery was breathtaking, and I would feel so close to God as I admired His work. One day, as I was driving along, singing to the radio, I felt a nudge to turn down an unfamiliar road. I had gotten to know the area quite well and had a particular route I would take most of the time. I had no idea why, but I felt an urge to turn left where I normally turned right. I was heading into unfamiliar territory but had a sneaky suspicion that something was up. I listened to my intuition, turned left, and began traveling down the winding road.

I drove for a while, but nothing really caught my eye. There were several homes and farms and lots of old, abandoned buildings. I wondered if this was it. I wondered why I had felt such a strong urge to come this way. Nonetheless, I wasn't on any sort of schedule, so I decided to just keep going. I drove for several miles before I came upon a little country store. There were lawnmowers and mulch for sale and signs that said "organic fruits and vegetables." I realized that I was running low on a few veggies and decided to pull in to stock up. As I turned into the lot, I noticed several woodcarvings that were placed throughout the property. There was an alligator, some bears, and what looked to be a huge totem with several different animals. *How interesting*, I thought. I just had to take a look!

I pulled in slowly, as I was looking at all of the different carvings on either side of the parking lot. I stopped my car and put it in park, grabbed my keys out of the ignition, and opened my door. As I lifted my head to get out, I found myself staring at one of the most beautiful carvings I had ever laid eyes on. It was a carving of an Indian chief. *Holy cow!* It was Chief Joseph. There he was, staring right at me. I got out of my car, walked up to him, and placed my hands on the wolf that adorned his head. My heart filled up, and I felt such warmth come over me. *Thank you for coming to me, Chief Joseph*, I said silently in my head. *I love you.*

Over the next couple of days, I found myself listening to Native American music and felt that Chief Joseph was close by. He let me know he was around me several times while I completed my respite in Massachusetts. Once, was while I was getting a massage, the therapist put on some beautiful Native American flute music. Another time, the chief made his presence known when I was visiting a nearby town with my parents, who had come to visit for the day. As we walked through a store that carried Native American clothing and knickknacks, I noticed a very ornate set of dishes. As I walked closer to take a look at them, I couldn't believe it. Written on a small card next to the dishes was the name of the design. That particular set of dishes was called "Chief Joseph."

I ended up purchasing the carving of Chief Joseph. It sits in my home where I can see it every day. I put my hands on it often and can honestly feel so much strength coming from it. I am so grateful for Chief Joseph, and I plan to never lose touch with him again. Thanks to my beautiful one-of-a-kind carving of him, I get a daily reminder that he is near.

Chapter 9

Connecting with Heaven

So now, I was able to connect with angels and animals and I knew one of my spirit guides. Life was starting to look pretty amazing again. I had decided to step away from seeing clients in long-term care for a while and focused my time and energy on seeing children. I was a contractor for the county I lived in and was carrying a full caseload. I would see children, birth to three years old, in their homes on a weekly basis. Since I specialized in the area of feeding and swallowing disorders, I often received referrals for children with more serious issues. My caseload was quite diverse, however, and I had several children on my caseload who I saw for speech and language concerns. I had such an amazing bond with the kids and got close with so many of the families. I found that as my abilities to "connect" on a spiritual level increased, my intuitive abilities did as well. I seemed to be able to connect with the children on a really deep level, and I was able to witness so many miracles, just as I had done with Jim in the rehab facility. When I would arrive for therapy, parents would often say that their little one had been standing at the door for the past hour saying "JuJu's coming," even when their parent hadn't mentioned a thing.

I remember one little boy in particular. His mom said that he would drive her absolutely crazy. He would stand at the door for hours saying, "JuJu's coming, JuJu's coming," over and over. She said he was so excited about me coming and would get all worked up until I got there. And he wouldn't leave the door. She was baffled and couldn't understand how he knew I was coming, as it happened even when we had switched from our usual days to another day. I had a sneaky suspicion what was going on, but I wasn't about to start talking to his mother about it. I just enjoyed the fact that the children and I were very connected and that I was able to help so many of them make incredible gains. The angels helped me carry out my task of helping those little light-workers, and I was grateful to be able to watch their transformations.

In 2008, a close and dear friend became quite ill and was preparing to transition up to heaven. Jean was like a second mother to me and I loved her dearly. She was one of the first people I met when I moved to Pennsylvania. I had met her through her son, Joe, a wonderful and kind man with a heart of gold. Jean and I hit it off instantly and we quickly became good friends. I was often invited to eat with her family for Sunday dinners, where I enjoyed great food, laughter, and a lot of storytelling. I so enjoyed the time I spent with Jean's family. They were an amazing group of people who loved life and clearly loved each other.

Jean was a feisty little Italian woman with a big heart. She was the type to tell it like it is, in her own loving way, and was the heart and soul of her family. Jean had a good life and a strong faith in God, and she never missed an episode of her favorite television preacher's show. She was full of spunk and had such a bubbly personality. Jean had lost her husband many years before and had never remarried. Occasionally, Jean would reminisce about their many camping trips, something they had enjoyed doing frequently with friends and family. I often wondered why Jean never remarried, but I got the sense that her husband was her one and only, her true soul mate.

One day, Jean began complaining that she wasn't feeling well. She had been coughing for a number of weeks but refused to see a doctor. Jean's cough got progressively worse, and she began to complain that she felt some sort of lump in her throat. Her appetite began decreasing, and within a matter of a few days, she was experiencing some difficulty swallowing. Jean finally made an appointment with her physician to see what was going on. The news wasn't good. She had waited too long. Jean had cancer of the esophagus and stomach, and her prognosis was poor. Her physician stated that there wasn't anything that could be done, that the cancer had spread too much, and that Jean's health would decline very quickly. We were all shocked and couldn't believe what we were hearing. How could this feisty, vibrant little woman who was so full of life be taken away? Jean accepted the news just as we would all expect her to, with strength and courage. It amazed me that Jean could stay so strong, or at least appear that way, knowing that she would soon be facing death. I realize now that she gave us all such a gift. Even though Jean had been given a death sentence, she continued to be that strong-willed, feisty little Italian woman we all loved and admired. She never wanted anyone to see her weak and she made sure that no one did, even to the end.

Jean entered the hospital, and her condition worsened quite rapidly over the next couple of weeks. It was difficult to visit her, and we all choked back the tears we so wanted to shed. Jean had made it very clear that she didn't want to see anyone crying for her. I can't tell you the number of times each of us had to leave the room so that we could honor her wishes. We would walk out into the hallway, let the tears flow, and then return after thoroughly drying them off. Jean never felt sorry for herself. She never showed any fear and continued to make us all laugh right up to the end. As I watched my dear friend deteriorate, nothing could prepare me for what was about to happen, as this was where my true awakening would occur, at the end of this beautiful soul's journey.

One afternoon, I went to see Jean in the hospital. She looked so weak and wasn't able to eat anymore. She would attempt to speak, but her voice was faint, and she appeared to be a bit confused at times. I went home to rake the yard and clear my head. I often spent time outdoors, with Mother Nature, to clear myself and get grounded, and I needed it more now than ever. My eyes began welling up with tears as I raked. I began to notice the sound of so many birds chirping and singing. They were so loud and I felt they were singing Jean home, while at the same time letting me know that everything was going to be okay. I began thinking about Jean, picturing her lying in that hospital bed. Was she scared? Did she feel alone? I asked the angels to go lay by her side so that she might feel safe and know that they were near. I asked them to make Jean's transition easy and to whisk her away to heaven when it was time. I felt their reassurance, and as I looked up at the sky, I noticed some sunbeams shooting out through some nearby clouds. I felt an overwhelmingly peaceful feeling come over me and I knew that everything was going to be okay.

As I continued raking the yard, something amazing began to happen. I began to see things in my head, almost like I was watching a movie. Jean came into the picture and I began seeing her lying in her hospital bed. Her eyes were closed and she was mumbling in her sleep. The movie continued to expand, and I began to see her husband waving to her from heaven. I had never met Jean's husband, as he had died a number of years before, and I had never actually seen pictures of him. However, I knew it was Oz, and I was able to see him clearly. He was calling down to Jean from heaven. He was telling her how wonderful it was in heaven and that he couldn't wait to show her everything. He had a mug of beer in his hand (yes, seriously), and I could hear what sounded like several voices laughing and carrying on. It sounded like they were having one heck of a party. I watched as Jean spoke back to him, telling him how afraid she was of not knowing what was going to happen. Oz reassured her that everything was going to be fine and that everybody was waiting for her. He was grinning from ear to ear as he motioned with his arm and said, "Come on," over and over. As quickly as my vision had appeared, it was over.

Wow, I thought. *That was incredible.* I stood there for a while trying to grasp what had just happened. It felt so real. I knew I had seen it. There was no question in my mind. I was completely blown away as I kept going over the whole scenario in my head, recalling every last detail so that I wouldn't forget. My tears of sadness soon turned into tears of joy, and I began laughing. I had just tapped into heaven somehow, and it felt amazing. I felt overcome with so much love. I knew that God was close at that moment, and I knew that He was taking care of everything.

I saw Jean's son, Joe, later that day and told him everything that had happened. I knew that Joe was a believer in that sort of thing, as he enjoyed hearing my many stories about connecting with the angels and animals. He seemed quite surprised about the whole thing and said that I had described his dad to a T. He even validated that his father did, indeed, drink beer from a mug! We both laughed for a bit in amazement and then came to the realization that Jean's time was drawing near. Our laughter turned into silence as we looked at each other and sighed. Although we knew that Jean was being watched over, the pain of losing her still cut so deep.

I received a phone call from Joe the next day. He had just gotten off of the phone with his younger brother, who had visited Jean the day before. Billy had spent the afternoon sitting with his mom as she lay quietly in her hospital bed. He said that at one point in the afternoon, she appeared to be having a conversation with their father. He said that Jean was mumbling things that were difficult to make out at times, but that he was certain she was talking to their dad. Joe and I checked the timeline and realized that Billy had been with his mother while she had that conversation with their dad at the same time I had seen that little movie in my head. We were floored! I'm sure you can imagine how big my eyes were as I listened on the other end of the line. I couldn't believe what had happened, and although it was something crazy and amazingly new, it felt so natural. We lost our dear Jean the very next day. She went peacefully, just as I had asked. The family said their good-byes, and we all felt a hole in our hearts. Jean's family had lost their rock.

There was a packed house at Jean's funeral. I sat in the front with her family, next to her son Joe. As the priest was talking, I asked Jean to give us a sign that she was there with us. I whispered to her son and told him that I had asked for a sign from her. "She'll let us know she's okay," I told him quietly. As soon as I had finished my last word, we both noticed some leaves suddenly fall from one of the flower arrangements sitting in the front of the church. Joe and I just looked at each other, our eyes wide as could be, and smiled at one another. We knew that Jean was sending us a sign, letting us know that she was with Oz and the angels. We joked later that day that Jean would never have missed her own funeral!

Since my initial awakening, when I was able to connect with heaven, I have continued to connect with Jean on a regular basis. I thank her often for being in my life and for playing such a pivotal role in my awakening. I tell her how much I love her and that I can't wait to see her in that magnificent place, and I ask her to help guide me on my path. She gives me signs that she's around often, and I can always hear her laughing and having a grand old time up there. She is surrounded with family and friends and continues to be that feisty little woman I knew here on earth. I love you, Jean, and I can't wait to see you again someday. Until then, keep lighting the way.

Chapter 10

My Journey Continues

As I embraced my new gift and began learning how to understand it and use it, I started to realize just how freaking amazing my new skill was. I couldn't believe how easy it was for me to connect with others' departed loved ones, and it was literally mind-blowing at times. I had been an empath my entire life and had always been able to feel what those around me were feeling. It wasn't something I necessarily wanted to do, as all too often, those around me weren't feeling the happiest. Something had changed in me, and all of my senses were being awakened or opened up now. I was able to hear things, feel things, and even know things that I would not have been privy to before. I was seeing clients on a regular basis and was receiving specific and unique information from their loved ones, angels, and guides. It felt so natural and was quite easy for me. Not only was I able to connect with departed souls and provide messages pertaining to past and present events, I was also somehow able to predict the future and would often hear from clients when the future events I told them about would come to fruition. Messages were always loving and supportive, and I can honestly say that to this day, I have never received anything negative. I give props to the angels for keeping it that way. I say it all the time: I would never do this work without having the angels involved!

As time went on and I began seeing more and more clients, my abilities seemed to only get stronger. I found a mentor and worked on honing my skills. I learned new things about myself daily and continued to be amazed at how my perspective about everything was changing so rapidly. Through it all, I remained so grateful for my abilities. I connected with God and the angels every single day, thanked them for allowing me to do what I did, and asked them to continue to guide me. I continued to ask God to let me see things through His eyes. To this very day, He has answered my prayer.

As I juggled my career as a speech pathologist and medium, I found it more and more difficult to separate the two. As my abilities as a medium became stronger, I found it difficult to turn my abilities off when in my speech pathologist role. I have always prided myself in not being a "nosy psychic" and know the importance of not tuning in to someone's stuff unless I'm asked to. As time passed, however, I found it harder and harder. I would often receive messages about a patient's diagnosis, especially if it was incorrect or if a piece of the puzzle was missing. I couldn't speak up and say anything about what I was receiving, as most of my families had no clue what I was moonlighting as. I asked the angels to help me to turn my abilities off if there wasn't anything I was supposed to do about a particular situation. Just as with so many times before, as soon as I asked, the angels answered. The messages and visions stopped. Not altogether, but the ones that would come that I knew I couldn't do anything about seemed to cease almost immediately. My intuition still played a pivotal role in my therapy sessions, and the angels continued to help as well, but I was no longer plagued with things I could do nothing about. That lesson was a valuable one! I learned not only to ask the angels for what I needed, but to be specific. It wasn't too long before I asked for their assistance once more. I asked them to help me in the same way in regards to receiving premonitions, as with my heightened awareness came a heightened ability to receive them. As before, I asked them to keep me from receiving premonitions if there was nothing I could do to change anything. I asked and it was done. I rarely receive them now, and I am all the better for of it. I can live with peace in my heart knowing that God has everything under control.

I continued working as a speech pathologist for a couple of years, but as my career as a medium began to take off, I took on fewer and fewer speech-therapy clients. My new business really started to grow as word got out, and I just loved my new career. I was changing lives, and it felt good. As business boomed, I realized that I needed to find a new home for my business. I had been traveling to clients' homes, just as I did for my speech clients, and I was getting tired. I was so tired of driving everywhere and felt ready for people to come to me. I was extremely busy seeing clients for readings and healing sessions, teaching classes and workshops, all while trying to maintain a full load of speech-therapy clients. *If I had a central location where I could see clients for my "angel work," my life would be a whole lot easier,* I thought. I decided right then and there that I was ready for my first place. I didn't know where it was to be, but I knew what I was going to call it: Guided By Angels. That would be the name of my business. I mean, if it weren't for the angels, I wouldn't have been where I was, and I owed them so much. That was truly how I felt: guided by angels.

I pushed my fears to the side and asked the angels to help. "Angels, please help me find the perfect place." I talked with them daily, asking for them to guide me to my new home. To be honest, I didn't even look for a new place very hard. I just didn't have the time. I would get online once in a while but felt overwhelmed with all of the possibilities. I asked the angels to take care of things and just show me where I was supposed to be when it was time. I decided to let go and let them guide me. I mean, I got this kind of stuff for my clients during their readings. The angels would surely come through for me. I let go of control and allowed the angels to lead me to the perfect place.

Over the next few weeks, I could feel some sort of excitement growing all around me. I knew that the angels were working on things and felt that they were getting my new place ready for me. I had no idea where my place would be but kept telling them that I was ready whenever they felt it was time. I knew that everything was being divinely guided. All I had to do was be patient and open for any messages or signs I might receive. One evening, I had a very lucid dream. I dreamt about a space in a neighboring town, one that was quite familiar to me. I had visited the space just a couple of months before to catch up with an old friend who was renting the space for her own business.

My friend was a hairstylist and had opened a shop where she made wigs for people with cancer. I hadn't seen her in a long time and decided to stop in to see how she was doing. She was eager to show me around her place, and I could feel the enthusiasm and love she poured into the beautiful wigs she made for her clients. I took some of her cards and told her that I would help spread the word about what she did. "You help so many people," I told her, and I hugged her good-bye. I had no idea that the angels had not only made me think of my old friend, but had given me the idea to go and visit her. The angels had a plan and it was unfolding right before my eyes, even if I couldn't yet see if for myself.

It was two months later when I had my dream about that space. I had waited patiently for the angels' guidance and continued to ask for answers. As usual, before going to sleep, I had asked the angels to show me where I was supposed to be. I often receive guidance while sleeping and frequently ask for guidance before falling to sleep. Like I mentioned before, on this particular night, I dreamt about my friend's space, the one I had just visited two months before. You can imagine my surprise that they would be showing me that particular spot. The space was already taken by someone I knew. When I woke the next morning, I told the angels that it just didn't make any sense. Yes, I often had conversations with them. I brushed it off and continued asking them to show me where I was supposed to be. "Please make it clear and concise," I asked before going to bed the next evening. I wanted to make sure I was being specific. Well, would you believe that I dreamt about the same place again? *Hmmm*, I thought. *I have no idea why you want me to go by there.* I began wondering if they were telling me that I was to share a space with my friend, but that didn't make much sense to me, as the space was very small. I had no idea what the angels were up to but realized that they were trying to tell me something. I decided it was time to take a drive over to my friend's place that morning, if for no other reason than to remove it from their list. "I'll go ahead and drive by it just so we can get on with things," I remember telling them.

The drive didn't take long, as my friend's shop was only about ten minutes away from my home. I sang along to the radio as I drove, without a care in the world. I was so sure that this was a wasted trip, but I wanted to drive by so that I would stop dreaming about this particular building. "I have no idea why you want me to drive by that building, but I am listening," I said. I finally reached the block where the building was, and as I turned the corner, I noticed that the sign that was once hanging outside was gone. I pulled up in front of the building and couldn't believe my eyes. The space was empty, and there was a sign that said "For Lease" in the window. I was speechless. I just sat there staring at the building, in shock of what had just happened. I knew right then that the angels had arranged everything. They had shown me this spot for a reason. I parked my car, got out, and, still in disbelief, peered inside the window. Everything was gone. I walked around to the front of the building where the landlord ran a floral shop. I decided to go in just to feel things out.

As I walked into the shop, I was immediately surrounded by angels. I mean, there were little angel statues everywhere inside that floral shop. There were all sorts of different shapes and sizes, and I walked around and gazed at each and every one of them. *This is a sign,* I thought. The angels were really trying to get my attention. I introduced myself to the owner and told her that I was interested in looking at her space in the back. I didn't even hesitate in telling her that I was a medium and that I would be using the space to see clients. I had no idea what her reaction would be, as this was really the first time I was coming out of the closet to anyone who had not sought me out, but I knew I couldn't hide anymore. She was elated.

"My prayers have been answered," she said. "You will fit in perfectly here."

The landlord took me to the back of the building to look at the vacant space. We discussed pricing, and I told her of my plans for paint colors and decorating. She was open to anything I wanted to do with the place and really seemed excited that I was there. "It's perfect," I said. We shook hands and planned to meet the next day to sign paperwork. Wow, the angels really came through. Not only had they shown me where I was to land, but they were literally everywhere inside of that little floral shop, making sure I knew that they had led me there. It turns out that the florist places angels in many of her arrangements, a special touch that she has been drawn to do for many years in the hopes of letting her clients know that they are never alone. I knew, as soon as I saw them all lined up inside of her shop, that this was the perfect place for me. I thanked the angels not only for leading me to the perfect place, but for teaching me to have patience while they took care of all of the details. Thank you, angels, for always answering my call!

I had so much fun designing and decorating my new place. I spent all of my free time painting, hanging curtains, and placing inspirational pictures and messages on the walls. I played uplifting music while I worked and knew that the angels were helping me create something magical. I enlisted friends who were more than happy to help me get my space ready. We could all feel the excitement building and knew that something big was going to happen. When I was ready to open my doors, I held an open house and was amazed at the number of people who showed up. There were lots of friends and clients who showed up, and I felt completely supported. I knew that something amazing was happening, and I was just grateful to be along for the ride. "Let me be an instrument of Thy peace," I prayed daily. "Let me help others however I can. Let me serve as a light upon their path." My conviction was strong and my commitment deep as I spoke with God. I knew that I had been given an amazing gift, and I wasn't about to take it for granted.

Chapter 11

Leaving My Post

As news of my new business spread, I got busier and busier. I started taking on more clients who sought connection with loved ones and angels and began to allow my speech-therapy caseload to decrease. Although I felt such a strong bond with all of my families, I realized that my time as a speech therapist, at least for now, was coming to an end, as it was getting more and more difficult to switch between roles. I was wearing too many hats, and my body was falling apart, literally. I still suffered many health issues that had yet to be diagnosed, and although I had found it easier to push through most days, the fatigue and body aches were beginning to win once again. I knew that something had to give, and I knew what that was. I couldn't save everyone, and it was time to make a decision.

The time finally came. I had to make a choice. I was getting well known in my area, and I knew that the people who worked for the county, who sent me referrals, would more than likely hear about my other job at any time. Although I never crossed any ethical boundaries as a speech pathologist, the fear of being "found out" was just weighing too heavily on me. I toyed with the idea of stepping down from my position as a speech therapist, but so much ran through my mind with even the thought of doing so. I felt such a feeling of obligation to my families and couldn't fathom letting them down. *Who would take my place?* I thought. *They just can't make it without me* was another favorite phrase my ego told me. It became like a battle within myself. I so desperately wanted to follow my new passion, but I couldn't seem to let myself let go. I felt as though I would be leaving my post and there was no one who would be there to take my place.

As I had done so many times before, I asked the angels for help. "Angels, if I'm supposed to only work as a medium, providing readings and healing sessions for others, then prove it to me. Show me that I can support myself completely, financially, by doing that work." Up until that point, I had needed both of my jobs to support myself. Well, that was all about to change, and all within a couple of weeks. The angels gave me my answer. My phone began ringing off the hook, and I could barely keep up. I was booked for weeks in advance, and people were asking me to teach more classes. I knew it was time. I had to make my mind up once and for all. It was hard to believe that my time as a speech pathologist was coming to an end. I struggled with my decision daily and found myself crying often. I felt like I was letting everyone down. I contacted my mentor, who helped me work through the pain and sorrow I was feeling. "But what will they do without me?" I asked during one of my many readings with her. She connected with my angels and guides, who came through with such messages of love and support.

"It's okay to leave your post, Julia. There will be others to take your place."

That's what they said, and that's exactly what I needed to hear. It was okay to leave my post. I sat there and sobbed as I felt a calm and peace come over me. I was releasing so much. The burden was lifted, and I knew that it was time for me to fly.

Chapter 12

Finally, A Diagnosis

As I soared into my new role as a psychic medium, my life began to take some amazing turns. I was led to begin yoga and quickly adopted a regular practice. Soon after beginning yoga, I started meditating on a regular basis. In the beginning, I needed guided meditation to help me let go of that noisy voice in my head. In no time at all, I was practicing silent meditation, and in much longer increments. Yoga and meditation would prove to play a pivotal role in me taking my body back, but it wasn't all I needed to win the fight. I know many people personally who have beaten illnesses and debilitating diseases with yoga and meditation, but, as hard as I tried, that would not be the case for me. I still suffered frequent migraines and neck pain, dizziness, and even vertigo. Sound sleep just wasn't a regular thing for me, either, as I struggled with insomnia on a nightly basis. Music would often get stuck in my head and I just couldn't turn it off. Although I know that is just one way we might receive messages from above, I soon learned it was also a telltale sign of what I had. My hands would shake from time to time, and my body would twitch every so often. My vision continued to move in and out of focus while little black dots would dance in front of my eyes. I still found that although I was doing all the right things, I was still sick. I'll have to admit, it was difficult not to fall back into the victimhood role, but I kept the faith and kept asking God and the angels for answers. "Please lead me to the right person who can help me," I prayed daily. "Please, please show me what to do." One day, after many sleepless nights and pleas for help, my prayers were finally answered.

I was talking with a woman one day who told me about a recent visit she had had with a naturopath. I had heard of naturopaths before, as I had seen other holistic practitioners in my area, but had never been to see one yet. The woman was raving about this particular naturopath and said that she had helped her when no one else was able to. I was curious and asked for the naturopath's name. Her name was Lynn Wright, and she had a practice just a short thirty minutes from my home. I called Lynn when I returned home and made an appointment for the next week. I was eager to see Lynn, as I was certain that the angels had brought her name into my path. I had been asking for help for so long, and maybe, just maybe, she held the answers.

The day of my appointment arrived, and I made the drive to Lynn's office. It was a sunny day, and the drive was a beautiful one as I made my way along the mountains. I hadn't received any sort of divine guidance about going to see Lynn, but I'll have to admit, I felt really good about going. I could feel some sort of excitement building up inside of me, similar to what often happened right before seeing clients before readings. I was familiar with this feeling, and it always meant something big was about to happen. When I arrived at Lynn's place, I noticed a big sign hanging on the outside of the building written in big, bold, golden letters that said "Angel Zone." Talk about getting a sign! I made my way inside and sat down in the waiting area. It was beautiful inside, and I felt right at home.

There were many things on display that were for sale, including lots of angels, crystals, and tinctures. Lynn came out and greeted me. She was friendly, and her energy was so calming and grounding. She asked me to fill out some paperwork before making my way back to her office. When I was finished, she led me back into her office. As soon as we sat down, I spilled my guts. "I've been sick for so long and no one can figure out what's wrong with me," I told her. Lynn nodded her head, and it was obvious she had heard this many times before. She described the procedure she would be doing and asked if I had any questions. She sterilized my finger and proceeded to do a finger stick, which was similar to when someone with diabetes checks his or her blood-sugar levels. She dabbed my fingertip on a slide and placed it under a microscope that was sitting in front of us. I was eager to see what we would discover.

As Lynn brought things into focus, I was amazed to be able to actually see my blood in action. It was still wet and "alive," and there were lots of things moving about. Lynn pointed out some of my red and white blood cells and lots of other things I can't recall the name of right now. She talked about each thing as she identified it, giving me her take on what she was seeing. She changed the magnitude of the lens several times during the evaluation, which brought different things into focus. At one point, I began to see what looked like little worms swimming around in my blood. Seriously, that's what they looked like. I pointed to a few of them and asked what they were.

"I was just about to get to those," she said. "Those are spirochetes, and you have a lot."

What the heck? Spirochetes? I'd never heard that term before and had no idea what that meant. Lynn went on to explain that when someone has a lot of spirochetes, it might indicate that he or she has Lyme disease. I instantly felt chills all over my body, which was one of my signs that something was "dead-on."

"I don't diagnose," she explained, "but I would suggest that you go see a Lyme-literate doctor to determine if that is indeed what you are dealing with."

My appointment lasted a good two hours, and I got a ton of information while I was there. Lynn handed me a flyer from the New York Lyme Disease Association and encouraged me to take a look at it.

"It has a short list of symptoms on the back. Check it out and see if any of them fit," she suggested.

I opened the flyer and turned it over to where the symptom list was and began to scan down the forty-three symptoms that were listed. "I have all of these!" I gasped. Actually, I had forty-two of them. One of the symptoms only pertained to men. I sat back in my chair and took a moment. I felt overwhelmed, but I somehow knew this was it. I had Lyme disease, and there was absolutely no doubt in my mind. I felt relieved to finally have some direction. I asked Lynn where I could find a Lyme-literate doctor. She gave me a couple of names, but I was drawn to one. He was located in New York and specialized in Lyme disease. "That's where I'm going to go," I told her. I thanked her for helping me and told her I would be back. I got in my car and drove home, thanking God and the angels the entire way. "Thank you for sending Lynn to me," I prayed. "Thank you for helping me get some answers."

I went to see the doctor in New York, and he was able to determine that I did, indeed, have Lyme disease. I won't go in great detail about my recovery, as that could easily be a book all by itself, but I would like to mention what ultimately helped me take my body back. Although I followed my New York doctor's protocol for an entire year, I continued to suffer from symptoms. It was exhausting and oh so frustrating and I found myself once again asking the angels for help. They answered and this time, it was the cure I had been praying for. The angels brought EFT (Emotional Freedom Technique), this amazing healing modality, to me when I began asking them for a miracle. I heard about it a couple of times and even purchased the Tapping World Summit program offered through TheTappingSolution.com. It wasn't a stretch to say that the angels were showing me my miracle. I just wasn't listening. My miracle lay right in front of me, in this big book with lots of CDs and scripts. I would often say, "Oh, I'll get to that one of these days," as I dusted the space where it sat on my shelf. It wasn't until I was having a new website built when it finally hit me that this was my answer.

My new web designer was working with me on pricing and branding, and because she noticed me struggling with a few issues, she suggested that I check into EFT. Now, don't ask me why this time seemed to bring on such clarity; it just did. I knew I was supposed to dive in, and I couldn't wait to get started. I pulled out my manual and began listening to the CDs while tapping along with the different speakers. I chose to tap for money the first day, as I felt I was blocking the flow of it somehow. That weekend, I made more than two thousand dollars in five hours, something I'd never even come close to doing before. I was hooked! I started tapping for health, specifically for my diagnosis of Lyme disease. I had been told that I would never be able to get rid of it, as it was considered chronic, and little did I know that those words were keeping me sick. My subconscious had heard that I would always have this, so it was sabotaging all of my positive affirmations and healing work I was doing on a daily basis. I tapped daily for my diagnosis, releasing it once and for all, and within two days began to be free of my symptoms. I continued to tap daily for a couple of weeks to ensure that I was well. And to this day, if I ever feel any symptoms creeping up, I begin tapping immediately. I have been able to completely get rid of my Lyme disease and any and all symptoms that came with it just with tapping. Tapping would help me in so many more ways. It has opened the floodgates to abundance in all its forms, and I can assure you that I will continue to tap for as long as I live.

I know that EFT was brought into my life for an even bigger reason. I had asked for a miracle and it had come. And I now had something to pass on to my clients who were suffering from their own illnesses and diseases. I was able to share this miracle with them. There was hope, and it came in the form of something that was so easy to do. Lyme disease was actually one of my blessings. As soon as I received my diagnosis of chronic Lyme disease, I began to be able to discern who else had it. I soon found myself surrounded by so many people who were suffering the same debilitating condition and didn't even know it. Many had been sick for so long that they just thought it was normal to feel that way. Many others had been misdiagnosed and were taking all sorts of pills to manage their symptoms, many of which continued to get worse. Now I had something that would help them, whomever they were. Diagnosis or no diagnosis, it didn't matter. Tapping had the potential to alleviate any and all of their symptoms. I have helped many people get to the bottom of what is ailing them, and I feel deep in my heart that this is one reason I contracted such a terrible disease. After finding my own miracle through EFT, I have been able to help so many others take their bodies back.

Chapter 13

The Woman on the Stairs

I finally had a diagnosis and was on my way to getting well. I began doing hot yoga three times per week, which helped me tremendously. I had a new man in my life, and I was beginning to feel like me again. It had been such a long time since I had felt so good, and I welcomed the light I felt growing inside. I was busy with clients and was adding more classes to my schedule as my energy increased. I just loved teaching others about the angels and how their loved ones were able to send them signs from heaven. It was a joy to get up each day, and I was grateful for the life that I was living. I was coming into my own, and I had hope.

My new guy was new to all of this. He had never encountered anyone who did what I did, and he had no clue what he was in for, but he willingly embraced all of me: my gift, my sensitivity, and my quirkiness. One evening, as Michael and I were sitting at his house watching television, something amazing happened. Michael was sitting on the couch in his usual spot near the kitchen, and I was on the other side of the couch, near the front door. I don't recall what we were watching, but it was a typical night for us, just relaxing at home. At some point in the evening, something in my peripheral caught my attention. I turned to my left and looked past the front door, toward the staircase that led to the upstairs. I couldn't believe what I was seeing. There was a woman walking down the stairs, only she wasn't walking. She was floating. I could see her as plainly as I could someone standing right in front of me, just like the little old woman who used to stare at me in the window while I washed dishes from time to time. She was light-gray in color and had rollers in her hair. She was wearing a nightgown and robe that flowed as she floated down the stairs. Her hair was salt and pepper in color, and she had a scowl on her face. I watched as she floated down the stairs and then down the hallway away from the front door. My face must've said it all because as I turned back toward Michael, he instantly asked, "What did you just see?"

I shook my head a bit and told him about the woman I had just seen floating down his stairs, describing her in great detail. "Her name is Mary," I said. "But I don't know where she's from or what she's doing here."

Michael stood up and replied, "Well, I don't know who she is," and made his way to the back door. We were expecting some of his family over for a visit and were planning to meet them in the backyard for a fire.

I sat inside for a bit and tried to get some more information about the woman I had just seen. "Angels, please tell me who this woman is and how I can help her." I felt that the woman hadn't crossed into the light for some reason, and I didn't want her hanging around with me. It was quiet. I didn't get any sort of guidance, so I headed out the back door to join the others.

When I reached the group outside, it was evident that they had already heard what had happened. Everyone was staring at me and asking questions. There were several close family members of Michael's present, and they listened eagerly as I told them of the woman I had seen floating down the stairs. I told them the exact same description that I had told Michael and told them that her name was Mary.

"She has a scowl on her face and rollers in her hair," I said. "She is wearing a housecoat and has salt and pepper-colored hair."

As I proceeded with my description of the woman, one of Michael's daughters yelled, "That's Mary from next door!"

Everyone started looking at each other in disbelief as they began to realize that I had just described their next-door neighbor who had passed away several years before. Why Michael didn't think of it is beyond me. I can only imagine this was all just a bit overwhelming for him, as I generally had a new and crazy story to tell him just about every day. Once his daughter pointed out the obvious, he agreed with her that it did, indeed, sound like Mary. I felt relieved. At least we had figured out who she was. Now, I had to find out why she was there, and how to get rid of her. That might not sound like such a loving gesture, but I was not about to share my space with some spirit who hadn't crossed over.

I headed back inside, telling the others that I was planning to clear Mary from the house somehow. At the time, I didn't have a lot of experience with helping spirits to the light, but I knew the importance of getting her out of my space. I sat down on the couch and called in all of my helpers. I called on Archangel Michael for protection and asked God to shine His light into and around the home. I called on Jesus and asked him to help Mary get to the light. As I connected, I began to understand that Mary had passed several years before, but for some reason, she had not made it to the light. She had simply moved next door, with Michael, and had continued going about her normal routine, in spirit form. I truly don't even think she knew she was dead. At least she didn't appear to know it as she floated down those stairs. Believe me, I know it all sounds crazy. At the time, it seemed a bit crazy to me as well. I had no idea at the time, but Mary would be the first of many spirits that I would come into contact with who, for some reason or another, had not found their way to the light.

I asked Jesus and Archangel Michael to go to Mary and let her know that everything was going to be okay. I watched everything happen, like I was watching a movie in my head. I watched as Jesus approached her and told her that she had passed so many years before, and that she had been stuck here walking aimlessly day after day. I watched as Mary began to weep, almost in disbelief at first, then shifting into a sort of understanding, knowing that what He was telling her was true. I watched as Jesus put his arm around Mary and began walking with her toward the light as Archangel Michael walked on her other side and offered love and support. I watched as they walked toward the light and as they began to float up to heaven. Mary's demeanor changed the instant she touched the light, and she no longer had a scowl on her face. She was smiling and glowing and she was full of beautiful light. I watched as loved ones who had been waiting so long for her in heaven greeted her. They had been trying for so long to get her attention, to get her to come and join them. They celebrated and welcomed her home with loving arms. I can honestly say that this was one of the most amazing things I had ever experienced. I felt so much love and compassion as I watched Mary be reunited with her family in heaven. It was magical, and I felt blessed to be a part of it.

I never saw Mary in spirit form again. After the clearing, Michael's home seemed a bit different, a bit more peaceful and calmer. Shortly after helping Mary to the light, a beautiful cardinal began appearing in Michael's yard, and although that was a few years ago, it still visits from time to time, chirping loudly when my birdfeeder has run empty. I giggle as I think it just might be Mary stopping by for a visit. From what I've heard, she could be quite demanding when she was living. That little cardinal showed up while I wrote this section about Mary, sitting in a tree overhead, chirping louder than ever. Although it might have been Mary telling me how to write her part in my book, I like to think it was her way of saying "thank you" for helping her finally find her way home.

I often see other souls, like Mary, whom I've helped get back home. They may give me signs that they are near, or I may be able to sense them waving to me from above. I can feel so much love and gratitude coming from them, and I know that they are helping me on my journey somehow. Being a psychic medium isn't always easy, and I can use all the help I can get! I just want to say thank you once again to God and all of my angels and guides who continue to help me on this journey. I am grateful for your unconditional love, guidance, and wisdom, and I am eternally grateful to be able to do this work. I vow to continue my journey and to be the voice of heaven. With gratitude ...

PART II

More Miraculous Encounters

Chapter 14

Our Feathered Friends

Over the years, as my connection grew stronger and I did more and more readings, I began receiving many messages of love and guidance for my clients in the form of birds. Since my very first animal communication came through and I connected with that little bird in Sedona, I knew that it was possible to receive messages through them, and I became amazed at just how often it actually occurred. So many of us receive visits and often guidance from loved ones, angels, and guides who choose to appear as these little feathered miracles. Here are just a few stories of how some of my clients were able to receive messages from their departed loved ones thanks to these amazing creatures.

~The White Owl~

I often hear about readings that I have done after the fact, through chance meetings. One evening, as I was preparing for a group reading, a gentleman approached me. He began to tell me about a reading I had done for his best friend's wife, Susan. He proceeded to tell me that I had connected with Susan's brother, whom she had lost a number of years before. According to Larry, I had received clear and valid information for Susan, allowing her to feel a peaceful knowing that her brother was okay. Larry went on to tell me that during Susan's reading, I had told her that her brother would come to her as a white owl. Now I'll have to admit, sometimes I wonder how the soul that I am connecting with is going to make certain things happen, but I've learned over the years never to hold anything back. I always share the information that I get, even if it sounds nuts to me.

The gentleman continued the story and told me that Susan couldn't wait to get home to tell her husband all about the reading that evening. She told him all of the details of the reading and also that her brother was going to come as a white owl. Her husband, quite the skeptic, laughed for a bit and told her that she would probably claim that every pigeon she saw was a white owl from that point on.

The next day, Susan went to pick up her six-year-old son from school, as she always did. As she waited in the doorway of his classroom, she watched as her son's teacher helped him gather his things. His teacher walked with him over to greet his mother. She told Susan how surprised she was at what had happened that day. The children had been given some free time to draw and color anything they wanted to. As the teacher continued to tell Susan what had happened, her son handed her his picture. It was a white owl. His teacher was astonished that he had chosen to draw it. Susan grinned as tears came to her eyes. She knew that this was a message from her brother, that he was letting her know that he was okay and that he was watching over her son.

I think you will agree that Susan's experience was absolutely amazing. During her reading, she was able to find out exactly how her brother would let her know that he was okay, and she was able to receive validation the very next day. As I always say, when we open up to unlimited possibilities, our loved ones will let us know they are near.

Here are a few more interesting stories of how several of my clients were able to connect with their loved ones through birds. I hope you enjoy them as much as I do.

~The Yellow Finch~

I did a reading for a gentleman and his mother. John Sr. had been gone for several years, but his family still missed him terribly. Although his widow, Margaret, had moved on with her life, she still felt such emptiness in her heart. When I arrived, Margaret and her son, John Jr., were anxious to begin. John Jr. had sat with me for a reading before, but his mother had never had one done. He had connected with his father during his reading and was eager for his mother to do the same. I started with a prayer calling in all of our angels and guides, and their reading began. John Sr. didn't waste any time and came through loud and clear from the moment I said "amen." He talked of his time in the military and offered specific details that only Margaret would know. Margaret began to smile as her husband reminisced about the time they met. He even brought up how he had to chase her in the beginning.

"He says you played hard to get," I told her. Margaret giggled and nodded her head in agreement. "He says he's with a bunch of his buddies who served with him," I continued. John Sr. even gave me the names of several of them, which I relayed to Margaret. "They're all sitting around a table up there, reminiscing about their time in the military," I said. He just keeps saying he's "with the boys," I told her. I felt that John was trying to relieve Margaret of any worry about where he was or whom he was with. She smiled at the news and confirmed that her husband often referred to the friends he had lost as "the boys."

John came through with so many loving messages that day. He spoke to his son, John Jr., and told him how proud he was of him. He thanked him for stepping in and taking such good care of his mother. "You were the best son anybody could ask for," his father told him. John Sr. talked about his grandchildren, whom he had only known for a short time before his passing. John Sr. showed me a picture of his grandson in his baseball jersey with the number seven on the back.

"Your dad is showing me a picture of your son. He's wearing a baseball jersey with the number seven on the back."

John Jr.'s eyes welled up with tears as he nodded his head yes, and he said, "That was my son's number. My dad passed away before he was old enough to play."

"Well, he's watching him now," I said, giggling. "He says that he never misses a game and that he is his number-one fan."

John Jr. laughed and told me that that was one of his dad's favorite sayings: "I'm your number-one fan."

As Margaret and John's reading came to a close, I told them that their beloved father and husband was going to come as a bird. "He's going to come as a little, yellow bird, like a yellow finch or something," I said. John Jr. laughed once again almost in disbelief. He proceeded to tell me that he, his wife, and their children had just started noticing a little, yellow bird in the yard a few days before. They had never seen one like it before and were wondering what kind of bird it was.

As John was finishing up his story, his wife came in the back door and said, "Honey, that little, yellow bird is out there again."

We all laughed, as we knew it was John Sr. popping in to say hello. Priceless!

~The Cardinals~

Cardinals are quite popular and a favorite for many of the departed loved ones I have connected with. Maybe it is because they are so easily spotted with their beautiful red feathers, or perhaps they were a favorite of the departed soul who is coming through. Whatever the case may be, loved ones who come through as this bird often do so in very creative ways.

I remember one reading I had with a gentleman who had come to connect with his father. During the reading, the gentleman's father kept showing me a red cardinal. "Your dad keeps holding it in front of my face," I said. I asked the gentleman what was so significant about a cardinal. The man laughed for several moments as his eyes filled up with tears. Once he was able to get himself together, he told me that he had just built a birdhouse with his grandson the week before. They had spent several hours on it, and when it was complete, they painted a bright-red cardinal right on the front of it. He said that he wondered at the time if his father had helped them put the birdhouse together.

"He was always building things," he said.

We both laughed for a bit. He realized that his dad had, indeed, been there the whole time.

***

I did another reading for a young woman who had lost her mother-in-law, Katherine. She was quite close to her and missed her terribly. I asked if she had noticed a cardinal, as her mother-in-law kept showing me one of the most beautiful red cardinals I had ever seen. She replied that she hadn't noticed one, so I told her to just be open that her mother-in-law would come to her as a cardinal somehow. "You don't have to look for one," I told her. "She will make you look when it is time." I received a message from the woman the following week. She had received her message! She told me that she, her husband, and their two children had been taking a walk one evening. They were just taking a walk in their yard and talking about their day when a flock of cardinals suddenly flew over their heads. They were shocked at the number of cardinals that had suddenly appeared.

"I've never seen anything like it," she said. "There was something like eight or nine cardinals flying all together. We knew instantly that it was Katherine, letting us know that she was okay."

Now, I don't know about you, but I have never seen a flock of cardinals before. How absolutely amazing that Katherine was not only able to appear to her loved ones as a cardinal, but she was able to do it in such a spectacular way.

***

So many of my clients receive messages through cardinals. Some have cardinals that visit every day, feeding from nearby birdfeeders that often appear to be looking in at them through the window. Some have even had encounters with cardinals who seem to be trying to get

73

their attention. I have one client whose husband comes as a cardinal and often pecks at her window. She always knows that it's her husband, Carl, letting her know that he is still right by her side.

~The Robin~

I remember a particular woman who came to me in hopes of connecting with her sister who had passed away the year before from cancer. Jane's sister had suffered terribly toward the end of her life, and she needed to hear that she wasn't suffering any longer. As I began connecting with the woman's sister, I heard the most beautiful voice.

"Your sister is singing to you," I said.

"She had a beautiful voice," Jane replied. "Everyone at church always commented on how beautifully she sang."

Her sister showed me a robin perched upon a tree branch.

"Your sister comes as a robin," I said. "She said that she sings to you often."

My client burst into tears and began sobbing. After a few moments, she told me that she had been noticing a robin for the past several weeks.

"It is always singing to me," she said. "It shows up everywhere!"

As her tears began to slow down, she said that she knew, somehow, that the robin was her sister all along. Now she had validation that her sister was still traveling beside her, giving her love and encouragement all along the way.

It never ceases to amaze me how our loved ones are able to come to us. Jane's sister is able to give her messages of love and comfort through the voice of a robin.

~Those Crows~

I met with a woman named Jackie, who had lost several family members. Many of them connected with her during the reading, including her mother and several aunts. They were all so different and came in with their distinct mannerisms and voices. One aunt in particular had a significantly rough voice. I saw her sitting around the table with the others, smoking like a fiend. I told Jackie that her mother, who was also deceased, kept waving her hand and complaining about all of the smoke while the other women around the table talked among themselves. There was a lot of chatter, and they were talking over each other, almost like they were competing to be heard. Jackie laughed wholeheartedly and said, "That sounds like them, all right." She said that her Aunt Mary smoked like a chimney and that her mother was always waving her hand and complaining about it. She went on to say that all of them tried to out-talk the others. "You could never get a word around that crew," she laughed.

As the reading continued, I began to see a flock of crows gathered in a tree. They were quite noisy, and I got the sense that they were trying to get Jackie's attention. I asked her if she had been noticing a bunch of crows lately.

"They are so loud," I said. "They just won't stop."

Jackie looked so surprised at what I had just said.

"Oh, my God, I've been noticing those crows everywhere," she said. "They won't shut up!"

I continued with what I was receiving and told Jackie that those crows were trying to get her attention.

"Your Aunt Mary just said that you'd better get rid of that bastard."

Yes, seriously, I had to tell my client that. Fortunately, she knew exactly what Aunt Mary was talking about. Jackie told me that her husband had a history of cheating on her and that she suspected he was at it again.

"He's just not a very nice person," she said.

"Well, your aunt obviously agrees," I replied.

Jackie said that Aunt Mary often used that exact phrase when she was still living, "get rid of the bastard," so she knew it was her.

"The crows are your family members," I told her. "It's your mother and all of your aunts. They're trying to get your attention," I said. "They're screaming at you. It's time to leave."

Jackie stated that she was ready to leave but just didn't know how. I asked her if we could say a prayer and call in all of her helpers, so that she could make a change. I called on Archangel Michael and asked him to stand behind Jackie, to help her to be strong and courageous. I asked Archangel Jophiel to come and be with her, to help her see just how beautiful she was. "You deserve better," I heard. I asked Archangel Raphael to place his hands on Jackie's heart and to help her heal from all of the pain she had endured, and I asked all of the angels to begin filling her up with love and light.

"Angels, we ask that you stay so close that Jackie can sense your presence during this time of transition." As the prayer ended, we opened our eyes and looked at one another.

"I'm ready," she said.

I was amazed at how her demeanor had changed. Jackie came into the reading looking so sad and broken. Now, she looked strong and confident, and her aura was so much brighter. She was glowing and seriously looked ten years younger. The reading came to an end, and we gave each other a big hug. I reminded her that she was being watched over and helped by the angels, but more importantly, she had all of those strong women in heaven paving the way for her. They would make sure things happened quickly and easily and would be opening doors for her. "Pay attention to the signs," I told her. "They will be coming in droves."

I heard from Jackie a few months later. She had finally done it. She had finally left her husband. She told me that things went so much easier than she had ever expected them to and that she finally felt free. She was beginning to be able to see herself in a new way, as beautiful, and she had even lost several pounds. It's amazing how, once we shed the weight of negative energy, whether it is a partner, job, friends, or even old negative patterns, we often begin shedding it physically.

I still see Jackie from time to time. Although she still experiences struggles like the rest of us, she is so much happier. Jackie still sees the crows once in a while. She reports that they are quiet most of the time, but that they tend to get noisy again when she goes back to any old, unhealthy habits. Jackie said that she looks up and says, "Okay, okay," as she knows that those crows are her loved ones reminding her of just how special she is.

"I've got one heck of a crew up there," she said. "I know they are going to make sure that everything turns out beautifully."

I just love how Jackie's family was able to come through so clearly. They were able to give her the messages she needed to hear so that she could make the changes she so desperately needed to make. And I will never forget Aunt Mary. What a character, indeed!

Chapter 15

Unlimited Possibilities

Before I begin sharing even more amazing stories, I'd like to discuss all of the many ways that loved ones, angels, and guides are able to connect with us. There truly are no limits. It is our own doubts, fears, and disbeliefs that can block us from realizing all of the miracles happening around us. People are all on their own journeys, having their own experiences, and living life with their own rules and preconceived notions. In my practice, I've come to realize that the more we can remain open to anything and everything being possible, the more we are likely to experience miraculous things. I have met countess people who have had miraculous encounters with their deceased loved ones. Some have seen their loved ones physically standing in front of them after they've passed, while others have caught a familiar scent that reminds them of their beloved. The scent might be flowers, perfume or cologne, cigarette or cigar smoke, or even a familiar body odor, as was the case for one mother I did a reading for.

Kate had lost her son in a terrible car accident just a year before we met. He was full of amazing energy as I connected with him. "He just bounces around all over the place, as if he's trying to make everyone laugh," I said. Kate validated that her son had been known as that type of person.

"He was always clowning around, trying to make sure everyone was happy," she said.

"Your son keeps showing me a football jersey with the number eighteen on it," I told her. Tears welled up in Kate's eyes as she nodded her head. "That was his number," she said.

"He says that you smell him when he's around," I continued. Kate began to laugh between the tears.

"I do smell that god-awful jersey from time to time," she replied. "I have always thought it was him." Kate said that she felt such comfort every time she smelled that sweaty jersey, for she knew, at that very moment, her son was near.

Although Kate had felt that her son was near her often, the messages she received during her reading only validated what she already knew to be true. Although things would never be the same for Kate, she had found peace in the fact that her son was able to let her know he was okay and that he would always be by her side. Why he chose the scent of a sweaty football jersey is beyond me, but Kate found it to be one of the best possible ways her son could've let her know he was okay.

Our loved ones and guides can connect with us in so many different ways. They can come as a bird, a butterfly, a dragonfly, and even a rainbow. They can come through in a familiar song, offering comfort and support, and sometimes even send messages of love and guidance through lyrics. They can send feathers and coins for us to find on our path and can even appear in the clouds that float in the sky. I cloud-watch regularly and am floored at how many loved ones and guides come through as I watch. I've spoken with a number of people who have witnessed the same phenomenon, most of them afraid to tell anyone for fear that people would think they had lost their minds. Several of my clients have experienced connection through music. One client in particular comes to mind.

Elaine had lost her husband eighteen years before we met. He had died unexpectedly while she was driving them to an appointment, and up until the time of her reading with me, Butch had remained rather quiet. Elaine had only had one dream about her husband shortly after his passing, and that was it. She said she had never been able to connect with him since that initial dream, and she wondered why she hadn't heard from him over the years. It had been eighteen long years, and Elaine longed to hear from her beloved Butch. As Elaine's reading began, I was able to connect with him quickly.

"He's sort of quiet," I told Elaine.

To be honest, Butch was a lot quieter than I was used to. It was like pulling teeth to try and get him to say something. I received some messages for Elaine during her reading, but not the usual windfall that I was accustomed to. As the reading progressed, I asked the angels to open the floodgates so that Butch could come in loud and clear. I sometimes do this if I feel things aren't going as smoothly as I expect them to, and as always, the angels answered my call.

"Your husband says he is going to come to you through music," I told her. "I have no idea what that means, but he says that you will know that it is him," I added.

Elaine seemed open to the idea and said that she welcomed any way that Butch was able to let her know that he was still with her somehow. Elaine's reading continued, and she received messages from friends who had passed, as well as several angels. They offered guidance as to how best for Elaine to proceed on her spiritual path. They gave her books to read and exercises to do and promised that they would all help her get more connected to them. Elaine's reading came to an end, and I wished her well. I wondered if it had been helpful and asked the angels to stay by her side.

"Angels, please help Elaine get her sign from her husband," I prayed. And with that, I let it go.

Elaine contacted me several weeks later for another reading. She told me that she had, indeed, received a message from her husband, Butch. And it was through music just as I had said it would be. Right after her last reading with me, Elaine met with a close friend and told her everything that had happened. "Butch said he was going to come through music somehow," she told her. As the two friends continued talking that evening, Elaine told her friend how she suffered from insomnia. It had been going on for some time, and Elaine was desperate to find something to help her sleep. Her friend suggested that she listen to a particular New Age station that was offered through her cable provider in the hopes that it might help her relax and fall asleep.

Elaine decided to try it, since she had run out of any other options. That evening, Elaine put on the New Age station that her friend had suggested, lay quietly in bed, and closed her eyes. While she lay there trying to fall asleep, she said that she began to hear the most beautiful song she had ever heard.

"I mean, it was absolutely beautiful," she told me. After a few moments, she decided to open her eyes and see who the artist was. "I was so taken with the song that I wanted to write down the composer and order a CD or something."

As she opened her eyes and began to focus on the screen, Elaine was astounded to see the name of the composer. It was a familiar name: Hilary Stagg. The artist was someone that she and her husband listened to often when he was alive. They had even owned several of his CDs, which Elaine said she had never listened to since her husband's passing.

"I couldn't bring myself to listen to them after he died," she said. "I still have them in a box in the basement." Elaine said that she felt such peace and calm come over her. She knew that Butch was reaching out to her, letting her know that he was with her at that very moment.

I've done several readings for Elaine since that initial one. Although Butch has found many ways to connect with Elaine, she says that he often plays a Hilary Stagg song when she asks him to help her fall to sleep. What a beautiful thing!

It is truly amazing how the universe works to put things in order. As soon as Elaine's husband said that he would be coming to her through music, all of the little synchronicities began occurring to make it happen, like when her friend suggested that she listen to a particular New Age channel to help her fall asleep. That, my friend, is the universe at work, creating miracles.

***

Loved ones can appear in amazing and magical ways in nature. As I said before, there are no limits to what is possible. I spoke with one woman who received a sign from her father through a tree. This particular tree had been in the woman's yard for years, and she had never noticed anything unusual about it before. However, right after her father's passing, she noticed something different about the tree as she walked by it, something she did every single day. On this particular day, as she walked by that very familiar tree, something caught her eye. She walked up to the tree to get a closer look, and as she did, she couldn't believe her eyes. There, right in front of her, was her father's face. It was right there, on the tree. She was stunned, to say the least, and quickly told her siblings and other family members about what she had seen. They all came over to take a look for themselves, and they all agreed: it was his face. I can only assume it was his way of letting his family know that he would continue watching over them as that majestic tree standing tall and strong.

Clients often ask me, "Why can't I see my loved one?" as so many wish to see them physically standing in front of them. Many of the people I have met ask for this day in and day out but never get their wish. I just don't have the answer to that. I don't know why some people are able to see their loved ones, while others are not. My advice is always the same: to be open to so much more. If you long to see your loved one in physical form, you could be missing out on so many other ways that he or she might be connecting with you. Miracles could be occurring all around you and you might not even know it. Your loved one might be the cardinal or blue jay that sits outside your window. He might be the bird that sings to you each morning as you walk to your car, or possibly even a black bird that tries desperately to get your attention. She could be appearing in the clouds, just waiting for you to look up, or she may come as a beautiful rainbow, letting you know that there truly is a pot of gold waiting on the other side. Speaking of rainbows reminds me of a really cool reading that I did with two sisters. As I always say, signs can come in amazing and miraculous ways.

I met with two sisters who had lost their mother many years before. They were quite young when she passed and essentially had to raise themselves. Their mother connected with us immediately and spoke of the many ways she had come to them over the years: as a robin for one of the girls and a cardinal for the other. She came to them in their dreams, which they both validated as happening quite often. She often whispered supportive and loving words in their ears, which they experienced as gentle ringing. She even said that she came as an orb, which her daughters validated.

"She's been in several family pictures," one of them said.

As their reading continued, I paused for a moment and began to draw a rainbow on the paper in front of me. "Your mother comes as rainbows," I said. "I mean, they are everywhere!"

Both women gasped as tears began to pool in their eyes.

"My son is obsessed with rainbows," one of them said. "He draws them all the time. I have them all over my house," she continued.

"The rainbows are your mother's way of letting you know she is watching over him," I replied. "She is one of his guides. Your mother says that you always wish she could have met him. She wants you to know that she didn't miss out on a thing. She plays with him all the time and will continue to help him on his journey."

The women were so glad that their mother knew of her precious grandson. They found relief knowing that their mother would be helping him on his journey as he found his way toward that pot of gold waiting on the other side of the rainbow.

***

I spoke earlier about seeing my first full apparition, Mary, floating down the stairs one evening while I was watching television. Although Mary was my first encounter with a spirit who had not yet crossed over, she definitely would not be my last. The next story is about a little boy whose mother contacted me for a house-clearing. Her son was extremely sensitive and had the gift of seeing spirits. One spirit in particular was proving to be quite a nuisance.

Chapter 16

The Cowboy

I met Amy through my boyfriend, Michael. Although she was Michael's niece, Amy and I would become the best of friends. Amy was quite open to the idea of being able to connect with spirits and angels, as she had always had the ability to see, hear, feel, and sense things around her. Amy's ability had opened up at a much younger age than mine had, and she had countless stories involving spirit activity. She even had the gift of being able to see angels in physical form. Although Amy had the ability to connect with spirits, she was troubled by something her five-year-old had been experiencing for several weeks. For some reason, Amy hadn't been able to put her finger on what was going on with her son, so she reached out to me for help. Kyle often spoke of a man that would bother him at night. He would wake him at different times during the night, and it was beginning to affect Kyle in many ways. He woke exhausted and would often become moody and act out, something that was unusual for sweet, little Kyle. Amy was growing more and more concerned as Kyle's sleepless nights continued, and she asked if I would come to her house to see if I could help.

I arrived at Amy's home a few days later. On my ride there, I asked Archangel Michael to surround me with his purple light of protection, something I did regularly. I asked God to shine His light in and around Amy's home and asked Him to surround me with a light of protection as well. I felt an uneasy feeling as I pulled up in front of Amy's house, and I knew instantly that there was something there that didn't belong. I prayed for guidance and asked that things be cleared quickly, easily, and effortlessly. I summoned all of my angels and headed toward the house.

Amy greeted me as I approached the front door. Her son, Kyle, was at school, which would make it so much easier for us to talk about things. He was only five at the time, and we in no way wanted to instill any fear in him. He had a gift, and we wanted to support his amazing abilities. As soon as I walked into Amy's house, I immediately felt heaviness in my chest and a lot of pressure in my head. I made my way through the living room and into the dining room, where we sat down to talk for a bit. Amy began telling me about some of her experiences with paranormal activity. She explained that she had experienced many strange occurrences ever since she had moved into her current home. She explained how things would sometimes move on their own, like a spoon she saw stirring all by itself in a cup of coffee one day. She also often heard noises that would occur throughout the house with no logical explanation. Amy felt as if something or someone was constantly around her, but she never really knew who or what it was. Now, let me just tell you that I was not too happy to be hearing about all of this crazy stuff. I was new to this sort of thing, and I really didn't want to see anything move by itself. I had only cleared my own home and hadn't yet begun doing it for others. I remember asking the angels quietly in my head to ensure that nothing crazy happened while I was there. Although I was a bit freaked out about what I was hearing, I stayed put and let Amy continue with her story. I did, however, remind Archangel Michael to stand very close to me, as I was treading in unfamiliar waters.

Amy continued describing several more instances where she felt spirit activity was involved. She said that her son, Kyle, often talked of things coming and going as if they were floating in and out of their house all of the time. She said that she suffered from frequent migraines and occasionally felt sad or angry with no explanation.

"I sometimes don't even feel like myself," she said. "The anger and sadness comes on so suddenly and is overwhelming at times," she continued.

I knew exactly what Amy was talking about, as I had experienced some of those things myself when uncrossed spirits were near. I knew that Amy needed help, and I knew that I was just the person to help her. Although this was all fairly new to me, I knew that I was in this home for a reason, and I knew that I could help.

Amy and I sat down at the kitchen table, and I said a prayer. This was my way of opening up my "channels," if you will, letting the universe know that I was ready to receive divine guidance, and it is something I do to this day. I called on Jesus and Archangel Michael and asked them to surround us with protection and healing light. I called on God and asked Him to shine His light down upon us and in and around Amy's home. As I finished my prayer and opened my eyes, my head began to hurt. I felt a massive headache coming on and instantly heard the name Mary over and over in my head. I began seeing an older woman walking around aimlessly. She was bleeding from her head and appeared to be completely confused. She wasn't in any pain, just very distraught and walking around the room in circles, calling out for help. She didn't know where she was, and she didn't know what to do. I'm not sure if she even knew she was dead. I told Amy what I was seeing as it unfolded. We both tuned into her and felt so much compassion for the woman. Although we had no idea who she was or where she had come from, we wanted desperately to help her find her way home.

I called on Archangel Michael and Jesus and asked them to go to the woman. "Please give her some comfort and let her know that you are with her," I prayed. I asked God to continue to shine His light so bright so that Mary would be able to find her way. I watched as Jesus and Archangel Michael approached Mary, and I saw an instant sense of relief come over her face as they each took her by the hand. She smiled at the both of them as she realized she wasn't alone any longer. Jesus and Archangel Michael began guiding Mary to the light, and a complete sense of calm seemed to wash over her. She smiled at each of them as if to say thank you as they gently guided her to the light. As soon as they entered the light, I watched as they all began to float up toward heaven. Mary's loved ones were waiting with their arms stretched open wide. They had been waiting for so long. As I watched this amazing thing happen right in front of my eyes, the pain in my head began to subside. I felt a sense of peace wash over my body and the room, which had felt so heavy before, felt so much lighter. Amy and I both had tears in our eyes as I relayed what I saw happening. We just sat there for a few moments, looking at each other and smiling as tears rolled down our cheeks. We knew we had just witnessed something so magical and so loving, and we felt blessed to have been a part of it.

After a few moments, we began discussing the main reason I had been asked to Amy's home. We needed to get to the bottom of whatever was happening in Kyle's room, so we headed to the second floor. The stairs leading to Kyle's room felt strange to me, and I got a sense that this was where things would come and go.

"They use the stairs," I said. "But it's angels, too, not just spirits."

Amy nodded her head and said that she had seen several things moving up and down the staircase over the past several years.

"I never feel scared," she said. "I just know they're here using this as some sort of passageway or something," she added.

As we made it to the top of the staircase and into Kyle's room, I felt an eerie feeling. I felt uneasy entering his bedroom, which, for me, was usually a sign that there was something there that didn't belong. I sat on the side of his bed and just allowed things to come in. I opened up to any guidance that my angels and guides had to give me. "Please show me what's here," I prayed. As I began to receive guidance, I instantly felt drawn to Kyle's closet, which was located to the left of his bed.

"There's a man watching us from the closet," I said, as I described him in detail. "He's tall and slender and has a cowboy hat on. He has a piece of straw in his mouth. He pulls it out from time to time and spits."

Amy looked stunned. She sat there for a moment almost in disbelief and then said, "Kyle is always complaining about the man in his closet … who spits on him."

Oh, my God! I couldn't believe it. We both stared at each other with big eyes. I quickly tuned back in to see what else I could get about the man.

"I don't feel that he means any harm. He just finds it amusing to annoy Kyle from time to time."

Regardless of his intentions, we both agreed that he didn't need to be there. I called on Jesus and Archangel Michael and asked them to help the man find his way home to the light. I watched as Archangel Michael appeared to be scolding the man for bothering little Kyle. The man was chuckling about all of it. He followed Archangel Michael into the light, chewing on that piece of straw the whole way. I watched as he floated up, into the clouds, and into the bright lights above. He was gone, without a hitch. I had asked for things to be cleared quickly, easily, and effortlessly, and the angels had answered my call. I thanked Jesus, Archangel Michael, and my angels for taking care of things so easily.

Once the man was gone, I was guided to tell Amy about Archangel Michael and how he could help her son. I told her that he was the angel who protects us and that children really resonated with him. "Archangel Michael is ready to help any of us who call on him," I said. "And he really loves children." I expressed the importance of teaching Kyle to ask Archangel Michael for help anytime he felt scared. I encouraged her to find a picture of Archangel Michael and told her she would be able to find many pictures online.

"Find one that Kyle likes and print it out," I said. "Place it near his bed, and encourage him to talk to Archangel Michael every morning and every night and ask him to watch over him." I often tell parents to begin introducing their children to Archangel Michael, as he has the ability to make them feel safe within a moment's notice.

I connected with Jesus and Archangel Michael and asked if there was anything else that needed to be done. I immediately heard, "All is well," a message that I often received from Archangel Michael, letting me know that a space was clear. I offered a closing prayer, thanked all of our helpers, and asked the angels to continue watching over Amy and her family. I did a final walk-through of Amy's home by myself. It felt so much lighter. I no longer felt the heaviness that I had felt upon entering her home, and it felt so full of love and light. I was grateful for my experience there in Amy's home, and I was even more grateful to be able to help someone in need.

I heard from Amy a few days later. She told me that she had found pictures of Archangel Michael as well as Archangel Raphael and had hung them over her son's bed. She decided to hang some over her younger daughter's bed as well. Amy said that as she was hanging the photos of Archangel Michael and Raphael, her daughter, Isabella, walked into the room and waved at them. As she waved, she said, "Oh, hi!" as if she was seeing some old friends. Amy also reported that Kyle was no longer complaining about the man in his closet, and when she asked if he was still bothering him, Kyle replied, "Nope, he's gone." Amy says that Kyle has slept peacefully since that day. She gives credit to Archangel Michael, as she knows that he continues to watch over them each and every day.

I just love the fact that Amy's younger daughter, Isabella, who was just two years old at the time, seemed to recognize the Archangels Michael and Raphael. She was still young enough to remember them, as her connection to the realms above had not yet been hampered by fearful thoughts. We all have that amazing connection upon entering this world. We remember where we came from, and we remember God and the angels. Then life begins, and it is only through one fearful thought after another that we begin building those walls of doubt, fear, and disbelief. We begin to forget who we are and where we came from, and we often end up feeling alone and sometimes isolated. When we are ready to regain that connection once again, Archangel Michael is ready to help us—ready to help us release our fears. He will protect us and help us feel safe as we move forward into divine love and light once again. He will help us gain courage and strength as we dismiss any self-limiting thoughts and beliefs.

I've counseled many families on the importance of teaching their children about Archangel Michael and getting them into the habit of calling him in to help them daily. Children often recognize him, like little Isabella did when his picture was placed beside her bed. Teach your children about Archangel Michael and all of the amazing things that he can help them with. Encourage them to ask him for protection day and night, as he is ready and willing to protect all of us at any time. My life changed in miraculous ways when I began calling on this beloved angel to help me on my path. He continues to amaze me each and every day!

Chapter 17

A Present from Daddy

I had been doing readings for about five years when I was asked to do one for a young girl who was turning thirteen years old. I had never done a reading for anyone that young before, and I will have to admit, I was extremely nervous. I knew that Nicole wanted to connect with her father, whom she had lost when she was just a toddler, but that was all I knew. I didn't know anything else about her or her father, not even his name. All I had been told was that her mother was desperate to find someone who could help Nicole connect with her father, as she knew that she missed him terribly. Nicole's godmother, who was a friend of mine, contacted me. She was aware of my abilities and asked if I would be willing to speak with Nicole, to try and help her any way that I could. Although I was extremely nervous at the thought of reading someone so young, I happily agreed.

As the day of Nicole's reading grew closer, I found myself getting more and more nervous. I was quite surprised at all of the butterflies I felt in my stomach, as I hadn't experienced them to such a degree in a very long time. The feeling brought back memories of when I had begun doing readings several years before. It took me a few years to get over my own nerves when I started doing this work, but I had learned to quiet those butterflies as I learned to trust in my connection.

On the day of Nicole's reading, I began to focus on her as soon as I woke up. I generally didn't do that for upcoming appointments, but I can only assume that my nerves were playing a part in it. As I said,

Nicole was the youngest person I had ever done a reading for, and I didn't want to let her down. I felt that I needed ample time to receive information and wanted to give her dad as much time as he needed to come through. I asked for her angels and guides to come through loud and clear and to provide messages that would help her heal and allow her to know that she was not alone. I knew nothing of Nicole's father and had no details about his death, except that he had passed away when she was quite young. I called on him throughout the day and told him to come through loud and clear. "Please, help me help your daughter," I said. "Come through with whatever she needs right now, and make it crystal clear so that I don't miss anything," I continued.

As the day went on, I began receiving messages for Nicole. Many of the messages came in the form of visions in my head. During one of the visions, I saw a rose quartz pendant. It surprised me, as the pendant I was seeing looked just like several pendants I had recently purchased online. I had been searching for a rose quartz pendant for myself for quite some time and spotted the perfect one while shopping online one day. It was so inexpensive, I felt the urge to buy several. I didn't know why I felt the urge to buy so many until the day of Nicole's reading. Now it was all making sense. After he showed me one of those rose quartz pendants, Nicole's father asked me to give one to her when I saw her later that night. I gladly agreed and quickly went upstairs to locate them. I had no idea why he wanted me to give Nicole a necklace, but I was more than happy to follow his wishes.

As the time for Nicole's reading grew near, I could feel the excitement growing inside me. I was so nervous, I thought I was going to puke. As I drove to her home, I found myself calling on my angels more than ever. "Angels, please help me be a clear channel tonight. Please help me help this young girl however I can. Thank you in advance!" As I pulled into the driveway, Nicole's mother and godmother greeted me. They both looked extremely excited and nervous. I smiled at both of them, reassuring them, and maybe even myself, that everything was going to be okay. We walked inside and I was greeted by one of the most beautiful young women I had ever met. Nicole had a presence about her, such a loving energy, and was smiling from ear to ear. I literally remember her bouncing from the living room to the dining room, as her energy was just so high. She was so excited and couldn't wait to get started. Little did she know, I was shaking like a leaf inside.

I silently asked the angels to help me stay calm and relaxed as we headed into the dining room, where Nicole's reading would take place. I gave Nicole some simple directions and we bowed our heads in prayer. I asked all of our angels, guides, deceased loved ones, and God to come forward with messages of love, healing, and guidance for Nicole and asked that our hearts and minds remain open to receiving. Nicole's father didn't waste any time stepping forward. He was so excited to connect with his "baby girl," which was the first thing that came out of my mouth as we began. Nicole's eyes began to well up with tears as she validated that that was what he used to call her. Nicole's father continued as he told me that she had the ability to see angels.

"Your dad says that you can see angels, and he says that you recently saw Archangel Michael on your staircase," I said.

Nicole seemed surprised as she nodded her head yes.

"I did see him," she replied. "I was so excited to see him on my staircase, but I wondered if I was just imagining it," she continued. We both looked at each other in amazement, as we knew, at that moment, she was able to see angels. "Your father says that he called on Archangel Michael and asked him to watch over you," I said. We both smiled at each other as we could feel Archangel Michael with us at that very moment. He often comes through as a warm feeling, and both of our faces were turning red.

"Can you feel it?" I asked Nicole.

"Oh, my gosh, it's amazing," she replied.

As the reading continued, so many things made sense for Nicole. Her father came in crystal clear, just as I had asked him to. I had forgotten all about the necklace until about halfway through the reading, when I suddenly pulled it out of my pocket. I reached into my pocket, took the rose quartz pendant out, and showed it to Nicole.

"Your father asked me to give you this," I said.

Nicole burst into tears and began sobbing. It took her several minutes to get herself together enough to talk, and I was a little puzzled at how much she was affected by what I had said. As she choked back tears, she began to tell me about a dream she had had the night before. In her dream, she was with her father.

"It was so real," she said. She continued her story and told me that in the dream, her father had handed her a necklace. "But when I reached out to grab it, it slipped through my fingers and vanished."

Her dream ended at that very moment. I'm sure you can imagine the shock that came over me, and I think I remember picking my jaw up off of the floor at some point during her story. I was absolutely stunned. Still lost for words, I handed Nicole the pendant and said, "I guess your father found a way to get it to you after all."

What an absolute miracle that Nicole's father was able to get the necklace to her that he had shown her in a dream just the night before. Although that was miraculous in and of itself, the true miracle was yet to come. Nicole had lost her father at such a young age, and the pain and sorrow she felt had never gone away. I heard a short time after Nicole's reading that she had spent her entire life cutting herself. I can only imagine that she was cutting herself to lessen the pain of losing her father so many years before. She stopped cutting herself after her reading. I guess connecting with her father in the way she was able to was the healing that Nicole needed. Nicole was able to connect with her father and receive validation that he had never left her side. Nicole was now free from a lifetime of self-mutilation. That was the true miracle.

I spent time with Nicole, mentoring her and teaching her about energy, eventually attuning her to Reiki. Over the course of the next couple of years, many amazing things happened that Nicole and I were witness to. One of those amazing events occurred after another reading I did for Nicole. I don't recall many details from Nicole's reading, but I will never forget what happened just a short time afterward.

I did a reading for Nicole just before her fifteenth birthday. Her father came through, just as he always did, with so much love and support. He had guidance about current events in her life, as well as advice in regards to some things coming up in the future.

"Your dad is going to come as an orb," I told her. "He's showing me a picture of you, a close-up of your face. The orb will be right beside you, and it will be him," I continued.

I received a text from Nicole a few months after her reading. She had sent me a picture with the message "I got my orb" attached to it. It was a beautiful close-up of Nicole, and there was a rather large orb right by her face. Nicole reminded me that I had told her that her father was going to show up on her fifteenth birthday, as an orb. The day she sent me the picture was her fifteenth birthday. I was astounded and quickly replied, "How cool is that!"

A short time later, Nicole sent me another message. It read, "Oh, my God, enlarge the picture. You're not going to believe what you see." I quickly pulled her photo up and enlarged the screen on my phone. I seriously couldn't believe my eyes! It was her father's face, inside the orb. I was absolutely astounded and must've stared at the picture for several minutes. Over the years, I had read several different things about orbs and that there are sometimes faces inside of them, but I had never seen it for myself. I was amazed at what I considered yet another miracle that Nicole's father was able to orchestrate for her. I realized if he was able to do that, there was no telling what else he would be able to do for her. Nicole's father was validating for me that absolutely anything is possible.

I continue to see Nicole on a regular basis. She has blossomed into such an amazing young woman, full of love, kindness, and hope for the future. She is able to find peace and comfort as her father continues to come to her in amazing ways. His baby girl is now helping others, just as I was able to help her, as she has embraced her path to divine connection. Nicole is now using her own gift of connection to help others. She is destined for great things, and I feel so blessed to be a part of her amazing journey.

Chapter 18

The Truth about Suicide

I've met with countless families who have had to deal with the devastating loss of a loved one due to suicide. Although I have not personally experienced loss in this way, I know that it is one of the most devastating ways to lose a loved one. The pain, guilt, and confusion that it leaves behind can haunt family members for a lifetime. Those left behind live life with such a burden, wondering if they missed signs or could have stopped the act from occurring altogether. They often carry this guilt with them each and every day, wondering if their loved one is safe and, more importantly, if he or she is in heaven.

Many of us were taught that anyone who takes his or her own life is automatically banished from heaven, never being allowed in. After the countless readings that I've done where suicide was involved, I have come to a much different conclusion. It doesn't matter who the person was, how they planned and carried out the act, how angry they were, or how messed up they were. They are always taken directly to heaven. Multitudes of angels surround these troubled souls even as they begin to act upon their fateful decision. The angels know that they need love more than anything. They wait patiently to take them to heaven's gates, where they will teach them the error of their ways, and fill them up with love and light once again. I call it "angel school," as I see it as a time for healing and learning, with hundreds of angels acting as their teachers and guides. While in angel school, departed loved ones are shown alternatives to the decisions they made, allowing them to see how things could've been different. This isn't done as any sort of punishment, but rather to prepare them for their next journey here on earth, if they are so guided to return again someday. Every reading is different, and the time spent at this angel school varies from soul to soul. I'm not sure why times vary for each individual; I just know that they do.

The following story is quite an amazing one. I share it with you in the hopes that it might help some of you who are dealing with this traumatic and life-changing event. Names have been changed to protect the identity of those involved, and it is only with their complete blessing that I share their story with you. My wish is that you somehow find healing and comfort as you read their story. May you know that your loved one is in heaven, and more importantly, may you know that they are not alone.

I received a call from a close and dear friend one afternoon. I was scheduled to see her for a personal reading that evening. Ashley's voice was shaking, and I could tell that something was wrong. When I asked her what was going on, she proceeded to tell me that her brother-in-law had killed himself that very morning. I was absolutely shocked and lost for words, as I had known her family for a couple of years. I had done readings for her and her sister and had cleared each of their homes. We had started to build a close relationship, and Ashley and her sister were important people to me. Ashley began telling me a horrific story, of how Michael had walked out of the home he shared with his wife, Summer, that morning, walked just a few steps, and hung himself from the tree that stood right in front of their home. He had decided to end his life at seven-thirty that morning, the same time that everyone from his neighborhood usually left for work, and also the time when all of the children generally made their way to school. It wasn't a stretch to think that Michael was trying to make a statement. His own stepson was asleep in the house and was one of the children that was usually up and out the door for school by then. Not this day. This day would be different from any other. Ashley asked if I would meet with her sister, Summer, and the rest of her family for a reading that night. She hoped that I would be able to connect with Michael and bring some sort of comfort to her sister and family, to know that he was okay. I agreed and headed out to their home that evening.

When I arrived at Summer's home, I passed the tree where Michael had ended his life. Instead of feeling sorrow, anguish, and pain, however, I felt such love and peace. I saw fairies and angels dancing around the tree. They were working so hard to shift the energy around the tree back to a space of love and light. There were so many of them! The fairies were holding hands and dancing in circles around the tree, and the angels stood right behind them, singing beautiful music. It was an amazing sight to see, and I knew that all of Summer's helpers had come to her in her time of need.

As I walked into the home, I was greeted by Summer and her family. There was such sadness, and they were still shocked and confused. I sat down, gave my condolences, and quickly got settled in. I told everyone that we would be attempting to connect with Michael and any of his guides and angels, in hopes of finding out that he was okay. I said a prayer, asked for all of the family's beings of light to come in, and quickly connected with Michael's angels and guides. I saw Michael standing next to several angels. He had sort of a shameful look on his face and had difficulty looking in my direction. It was like he was so ashamed at what he had done and just couldn't find any words to express how sorry he was. Michael's angels spoke up and told me that he had done this act to cause harm, and that they were working with him to help him see the error of his ways. Michael's angels continued and told me that he would be in "angel school" for seven days, the place where souls, like Michael, are often shown alternatives to decisions they have made.

As the reading continued, more of Summer's family members came through, letting her know that everything was going to be okay. The angels came through with messages of love and protection and assured Summer that there was nothing she could've done. The angels assured Summer that they had been there all along and had intervened earlier that morning. "They made sure that no one came down your lane," I told her. Summer nodded her head, as if she knew what the angels were telling her. You see, as Michael hung from that tree, not a single car drove down the lane, as would usually happen. Summer and Michael's house was the first on the lane, so everyone had to pass it to get out to the main road. It was a weekday, and people were generally going by to go to work or to walk their children up to the bus stop. Not that day. No one drove by, and not one child walked to the bus stop. Summer's son, Robert, who wakes up at the same time for school every day, didn't even wake up that morning. He lay sleeping, even as sirens from the ambulance and police cars came roaring down the lane. As Summer told her story, we all knew that the angels had stepped in and protected everyone else on the lane from seeing what had happened. Celestial intervention had taken place, indeed.

As the reading continued, I told Summer that I saw a multitude of angels standing underneath Michael as he was preparing to take his life. They were waiting, patiently, to take him immediately into their arms. I saw Archangel Michael there also and told her that he had spared Michael any pain or trauma. Summer breathed a sigh of relief as a tear rolled down her cheek.

"Thank God he didn't suffer," she said.

I continued and told Summer that she would receive a sign from her husband in seven days, in the form of a feather. I didn't know where she would find the feather, just that this feather would be her sign from Michael that he was okay. That feather would be his sign to her that he had completed angel school. Loved ones often come through with signs, letting their loved ones know that they are okay. Summer's sign was going to be a feather. I went on to tell Summer that her son, Robert, who has the gift of seeing spirit, would see Michael after this seven-day period and would know that Michael was all right. I have to admit, when I receive the way in which loved ones are going to come through with signs, I always tell them they had better deliver! We ended the reading a few minutes later. Summer and her family appeared calmer knowing that Michael was in the angels' care.

I received a message from Summer exactly seven days later. She had received her sign. She had been cleaning out a closet that day and had come across a shoebox full of old photographs. As she sorted through the photographs and pictures, reminiscing about her life with Michael, she came across a large feather lying in-between two of them. She was surprised and instantly knew that Michael was letting her know that he was okay. Summer went on to tell me that her little boy had received his sign as well. When Robert got home from school that day, he told his mother that he had seen Michael. While Robert was sitting at his desk, Michael and Robert's grandpa appeared to him, standing in front of the room. Robert's grandpa visited him often, so this was nothing new to him. Robert continued to tell his mother that Michael and his grandpa were acting silly and making faces and that he had to keep from laughing for fear of getting in trouble with his teacher. When Summer heard her son's story, she felt a peace and calm come over her. She had always known that her father was watching over Robert. Now she knew that Michael was as well. She knew that Michael was in heaven and that he wasn't alone.

Summer was the one who found her husband. She still struggles with that vision, but with the angels' help, she has allowed herself to heal and let it go. She has come to terms that there is nothing she could've done to change her husband's destiny. He made his decision, and he carried it out. He was on his own journey and decided to end his early. Summer realizes that she may never know why Michael did what he did, but she does know that he is safe and sound with the angels in heaven and that he will continue to watch over her and her son.

If you have ever lost a loved one due to suicide, I am so very sorry. Please know that your loved one was surrounded by angels and was not alone. Your loved one was taken directly to heaven, where they continued to receive love and support from all of the angels. Let go of any guilt, and know that there was absolutely nothing you could've done to stop them from ending their life. Your loved ones were on their own journeys and, unfortunately, decided to end them early. The angels love them, will take care of them, and will never leave them. Ask for signs from your loved ones, and be open to the miraculous ways they can let you know they're near. They love you and want you to know they are at peace.

Chapter 19

A Flower from Grandma

I sat for a reading with a young lady named Sarah, who was in her early thirties. Sarah was seeking guidance about some important decisions she was facing in her life and hoped that her grandmother would come through to support her. Sarah received a plethora of useful information from her angels and guides—information that she said would be quite helpful, as she had some important decisions coming up. Sarah's grandmother came through as one of her guides and assured her that everything was going to be okay. Sarah said that although she knew her grandmother was watching over her, she didn't feel that she received many signs from her.

"I know she's there, but I just don't get any signs from her," she said. "I ask her to give me signs all the time, but nothing happens."

Just as Sarah was finishing her sentence, I began to see a lone flower standing in the dirt. It stood straight up, had white petals, and was standing there all by itself, surrounded by nothing but dirt. I told Sarah what I was seeing and asked her if it made any sense to her. She shook her head no and said that it didn't make any sense to her at all. I drew a picture of the flower and told Sarah that it seemed important and that it was somehow a sign from her grandmother.

"I have no idea what it means," I said, "but I know it's important. Your grandma says that it will make sense soon," I added. Again, it was one of those times where I found myself telling Sarah's grandma, *You'd better make that happen!* quietly in my head. Sarah's reading came to a close, and I handed her the sheets of paper I had been doodling on. We glanced at the flower that I had drawn, raised our eyebrows, and shrugged our shoulders as if to say, "Who knows?"

I saw Sarah a few months later while visiting one of my favorite local restaurants. I had no idea at the time that she was actually one of the waitresses there. I had never seen her waiting tables there and was quite surprised when she came walking up to my table.

"I got my flower," she said with a smile.

"You did? I can't wait to hear all about it," I told her.

Sarah proceeded to tell me that she and her husband had decided to landscape their entire front yard. They had turned up the entire yard and removed all of the old grass, and all that remained was a flattened yard full of dirt. They were doing some landscaping and planned to plant new grass very soon. Sarah and her husband had left their house to run to a local home-building supply store. It was midafternoon, and the sun was shining bright.

"We were going to pick up the grass seed and a few other items we needed for the yard," she said. "We were only there for about an hour."

Sarah continued with her story and said that when they returned home, they were shocked at what was waiting for them. As she and her husband pulled into their driveway, they noticed a lone, white flower standing straight up in the middle of their yard. Sarah said it took her breath away when she noticed it.

"I couldn't believe it," she said. "I just began crying. I knew it was my grandmother telling me that she was watching over me and that everything was going to be okay."

It is truly amazing that Sarah's grandmother was able to deliver her message of hope by way of a lone flower standing in the dirt. I've learned over the years that our loved ones can do some amazing things. All we need to do is be open to the miraculous ways in which they can deliver their messages. Ask your loved ones for signs, and try not to decide how those signs should appear to you. You might just block all of the other miraculous ways they can let you know they are near. Be open to unlimited possibilities and allow the magic to occur.

Chapter 20

Our Beloved Children

People are often surprised to find out that their unborn children act as guides for them here on earth. Many parents continue to grieve the children they have lost, not realizing that they have continued by their side, sending love and support. Whether children have been lost through miscarriage, abortion, or passing too young, they have such unconditional love for us, and they try desperately to let us know they are around. I often hear them laughing and see them playing in heaven. They are full of such love and joy as they explore their world up there.

Children offer such loving messages for their parents. Some simply want to say "hello" and "I love you," while others may offer profound and even urgent messages. I have connected with many children who have offered guidance in regards to health concerns, often leading their parents to the person who can help most. One subject that comes up often is that of infertility. I remember one woman in particular whom I had done a reading for. It came through during her reading that she had lost seven children. I remember being shocked at the number of children she had miscarried and felt the anguish she carried inside. All she had ever wanted was to be a mother. Several of her children came forward and said that she had a vitamin deficiency, but that the doctors weren't able to detect it for some reason. I can't recall the particular vitamin that was mentioned, but I do remember receiving guidance about the exact vitamin that was deficient at the time.

"It might benefit you to see my naturopath," I told her. "She's helped lots of people get pregnant when no one else could," I continued. I gave her the phone number and told her that she would be able to help her. "Your children are pointing at my naturopath, saying that she has the answers." The woman seemed to have a glimmer of hope and said that she was willing to try anything.

"I want to be a mother so badly," she said with tears in her eyes. "It's all I think about."

I heard from the woman about a year later. She said that she had visited my naturopath and that she did indeed have a vitamin deficiency that was keeping her from being able to carry her children to term. She had begun taking supplements and was thrilled to tell me that she had just given birth to her first child, a beautiful baby boy!

How amazing that this woman's children were able to come through and guide her to the right person who would help her not only conceive, but also give birth to her first child. As I write this, I can see all of her other children laughing and playing in heaven. They will be acting as guides for her and her son and will ensure that he finds his way in the world.

In my experiences, children who did not make it into this world due to abortion serve as a much bigger lesson than many realize. Abortion often comes with it such a burden of guilt, and many women carry its shame for their entire lives. Many quiver at just the sound of it and are quick to judge those who made such a difficult decision. As for the many readings that I've done, children who have been terminated always come through with loving and supportive messages for their mothers. I have met so many women who had to make this devastating decision within their lifetime, each and every one of them carrying such heavy loads of remorse, regret, shame, and guilt. Although most of these women come to me seeking connection with other loved ones, their children often come through with messages of unconditional love and forgiveness. Here are just a few of those stories.

I met with a young woman who had come to connect with her parents. They had been gone for quite some time, and Kim was eager to hear any messages her parents might have for her. Kim's father was the first to connect with me. I saw him as a big man with a big heart.

"I just want to call him Gentle Giant," I said. Kim's eyes began to tear up as she told me that that used to be what they all called him.

"He was such a big man with a heart of gold," she said. "All of us kids used to call him Gentle Giant." Kim's father came through with so many messages of love and support. He brought up recent activities that had been happening in her life, including her and her husband's anniversary and a recent wedding of a family member that she had attended. As Kim's father spoke, I began to see that he was holding something.

"Your father is holding a baby in his arms," I told her. "He wants you to know that he has your baby," I continued.

Kim began to sob. My own eyes started to well up with tears as I could feel the anguish she was holding inside. Kim began to tell me that she had terminated a pregnancy when she was very young. She said that it had happened long before her parents had passed away and that she had never told them or anyone else.

"I didn't want to disappoint my parents," she said. "They never would have forgiven me."

"Your father is holding your baby and just smiling at you," I replied. "He is so proud of you and says that he could never be angry with you." After a short pause, I continued, "Your father says that he'll watch over your baby until you are able to meet again someday. He loves you and wants you to know that your baby loves you too."

Kim's tears flowed for quite some time, and I could feel her energy becoming lighter and lighter as she released the burden she had been carrying for so long.

As Kim's reading was coming to a close, I saw two angels step forward. "There are two angels surrounding you now," I said. "They want to relieve you of this burden once and for all."

I could still see Kim's son giggling and squirming in his grandpa's arms in heaven.

"The angels want you to know how loved you really are. They want you to see the bigger lesson in all of this," I continued. Kim looked at me, a bit puzzled. "The angels say that this was one of the biggest lessons of your life. It was a lesson in self-forgiveness."

Kim and I both got quiet as we took in what the angels were telling her before I blurted out, "Oh, my gosh! You got pregnant with your baby so that you could learn how to forgive yourself."

I was speechless for a few moments, as I knew that this was the ultimate message. I watched as Kim's demeanor began to change. She was literally changing right before my very eyes. Her skin and eyes looked brighter, and she began to smile. She even had a glow about her that I had seen in many others who had been healed.

"You look like you are finally at peace," I said.

Kim replied, "I am. I am finally at peace with myself."

Kim hugged me tighter than I had ever been hugged before. She thanked me over and over and said that her reading had changed her life. Kim was finally free of the guilt and shame she had carried for so long. She had finally forgiven herself. I was amazed at the transformation that Kim had made in such a short period of time. I realized just how much our energy can be affected when we hold such a grudge against ourselves and loathe ourselves so deeply. Kim showed up at my front door broken, but she left with a newfound sense of peace and love. She knew that the baby she had chosen to terminate so many years before was safe and secure in her father's arms in heaven, and she knew that her daddy wasn't angry with her and that he loved her unconditionally.

Isn't it amazing how Kim's father and unborn child came through to guide her during her reading? They, along with the angels, knew the importance of Kim realizing her biggest lesson ever, the lesson of self-forgiveness. As I witnessed Kim's transformation before my very own eyes, I realized that forgiveness will truly set you free.

***

I met with another woman named Jeanie. She was a beautiful, petite, round woman full of love. I felt pretty certain Jeanie had never had a reading before, as she giggled nervously when I introduced myself. I felt her anxiety and told her that everything was going to be okay. "You will receive loving messages from your loved ones, angels, and guides today," I assured her.

Her energy shifted quickly into a more calm and peaceful state. She was still a bit nervous, but that's to be expected with someone who has never experienced what I do before.

"I always ask that you receive whatever you need the most for healing and moving forward," I told her. "Your loved ones, angels and guides know what that is."

I gave Jeanie a few instructions and moved into my opening prayer.

Jeanie's family members were so excited to connect with her. She had so many people come through that I almost couldn't keep up. I remember pausing and saying something like, "Wow, you have a lot of people up there." Jeanie's parents were the first to step forward. They were so loving, and I could feel all of the love and admiration they had for their daughter. In no time, there were several aunts and uncles and even grandparents who came forward to connect with Jeanie. Everyone came through with messages that made sense for Jeanie, answering many questions she had and offering messages of validation that they were able to see all that was going on in her life. As Jeanie's reading neared the end, I asked if there was anything else she wanted to know.

"Is there anyone that you wanted to hear from that you didn't?" I asked.

Jeanie looked at me for a moment and then said, "What about my children?"

I was actually quite surprised at Jeanie's question, as no children had come forward during the reading. I closed my eyes and took a few moments to receive guidance from Jeanie's angels and guides. I got her answer. As I opened my eyes, I asked Jeanie if she had two children, to which she replied yes.

"Do you have a boy and a girl?" I continued.

"Yes," she answered.

"Did you terminate two pregnancies?" I asked, to which she again replied yes.

"Your children aren't in heaven," I said. "They're with you."

Jeanie burst into tears. After a few moments, she told me that she had felt all along that her two living children were the same two children she had lost so many years before. She had known, deep in her heart, that her children had decided to come a second time. We hugged each other, and I could feel the relief that had taken over her body. Like Kim in the previous story, Jeanie's appearance began to shift immediately. She looked so much brighter and even looked years younger than she had just an hour before. She had been released of so much guilt, guilt that had been weighing her down for far too long. Jeanie thanked me and told me that I had changed her life. I assured her that it was she who had changed her life. Jeanie had made her own connection with the realms above and had entered into a flow of unconditional love that just can't be described.

"Just watch the miracles come flooding in," I told her. "Your loved ones, angels, and guides will be able to create miracles for you. Be open to unlimited possibilities."

Although the previous stories are completely different, with different outcomes, they are truly stories of love and forgiveness. We are all here, traveling on our own journeys, having different experiences. We are learning lessons, lessons that are meant to help us heal our souls. Sometimes the lessons we are supposed to be learning are far different than we could've ever imagined. Forgive yourself for anything that is weighing you down, and remember that you did the best you could with what you knew at the time. God loves you unconditionally and only wants you to love yourself in the same way. Ask the angels to lift any grudge you have for yourself. Surrender it to them, and let it go once and for all. Your children love you so very much and only want to see you happy and healed. The angels assure you that they will watch over your beloved children forever.

Chapter 21

A Grandmother's Prayer for Healing

I did a reading for a woman who had lost both of her parents. She was an only child and was absolutely devastated from their loss. Cindy looked tired and grief-stricken as I greeted her at my front door. It was apparent that she carried such a heavy heart. As I led Cindy into my dining room, where her reading would take place, I turned to her and said, "This is going to be life-changing for you." I didn't know why I was guided to tell her that, only that it was important for me to relay the message. As I began Cindy's reading, both of her parents came rushing in. They were so eager to connect with her and couldn't wait to speak with her, as they had so much to tell her. Cindy's mother began singing.

"Your mother has such a beautiful voice," I told her. "She's singing the song 'Somewhere over the Rainbow.'"

Cindy began to weep as she told me that her mother sang that song to her often.

"Your mother says that you feel all alone, but she wants to assure you that she and your father have never left your side," I said. Cindy's mother began talking about Cindy's son. "She's showing me a football game, and I see a young man wearing a football jersey with the number nine on the back."

Cindy validated that that was indeed her son's football number. Cindy's mother even spoke of a recent injury that Cindy's son had received during a game. "Your mother says that your son had some sort of miraculous healing occur after a football injury. She says that she sent several angels to help him heal from his accident." Cindy was shocked, to say the least, and it was apparent that her mother had said something profound. Cindy proceeded to tell me that her son did have some sort of miraculous healing occur, according to his doctors. He had sustained an awful injury that usually requires extensive multiple surgeries, but somehow, he had completely recovered in just a few short weeks.

"The doctors were baffled," Cindy recalled. She laughed a bit and confessed, "I knew my mother had something to do with it."

Cindy heard from so many loved ones during her reading. Her angels even peeked in and offered rock-solid guidance for some things she was going through.

"Your angels say that you're trying to make a really big decision. They assure you that what you are planning to do is the right move."

Cindy smiled as if she knew what they were talking about. As Cindy's reading came to an end, she began to look so different, like so many others I had been a witness to before. She had walked through my door a broken, grief-stricken woman, and she now looked so bright and full of joy. Her smile was so big, and I swear, I could hear little bells ringing every time she laughed.

"I haven't felt this good in so long," she said as she giggled. "I'm so grateful that my parents are watching over my son. They loved him so much."

As I walked Cindy to the door and we said our good-byes, I could see her parents, one on either side of her, walking with her as she went on her way. I can only imagine that once Cindy was able to connect with her parents on that blessed afternoon, they continued to send her signs to let her know that they would always be near.

Chapter 22

Fred and Ginger

I met with a woman who had lost both her mother and father. She missed them terribly and said she had been lost since their passing. Rachel's parents had been killed in a car accident and had left this world together. As the reading began, Rachel's parents came barreling in. They were laughing and dancing and having such a good time together. I chuckled and said, "They're like two peas in a pod."

Rachel burst into tears and said, "That's what everyone always said about them, that they were like two peas in a pod."

Rachel's parents were full of energy and were an absolute joy to connect with. As they glided across heaven's dance floor, they offered many messages for her, messages of love and hope. It was such a joy to watch them dance.

"They're like Fred and Ginger," I said.

Rachel once again began to cry, but she assured me now that they were tears of joy, as she knew her parents were so happy together.

"Everyone used to call them Fred and Ginger," she said. Rachel had so many family members in heaven. There were several uncles and aunts who came through for her, often providing their first name for recognition. Her grandparents came through, reminiscing about the past and providing clear pictures of the time they had spent with Rachel.

"They're all sitting around a big, round table," I told her. "They're talking about the good ol' days, and I can hear so much laughter."

Rachel validated that her family had often sat around a large, round table that her parents had in their home. They would talk about the good ol' days, and the laughter was never-ending. Rachel's father began to step forward and asked her to stop grieving them.

"Now you know that we are okay and that we are together. We wouldn't have it any other way."

Rachel's tears began to flow once again as she nodded her head yes.

"My parents were inseparable," she said. "I guess they just couldn't live without each other and that's why things had to happen the way they did."

I watched as Rachel shifted into a calmer, more peaceful place. The worry began to leave her face, her tears began to dry up, and she now donned the most beautiful smile. I could sense the relief that Rachel felt in knowing that her parents were still together. As Rachel's reading came to an end, her parents had one last message for her. "Your parents are going to come to you as a pair of cardinals," I told her. "This is going to be your sign that they are okay and that they will continue to watch over you." I asked Rachel if she had seen a pair of cardinals lately, to which she quickly replied no.

"Just be open to the possibility," I told her, "the possibility that they can come as a beautiful pair of cardinals."

I then told Rachel to continue asking her parents for signs that they were around and that she could ask them for guidance about anything.

"Be sure to call on your angels as well," I said. "Your parents can only do so much, but the angels can do anything."

I received an e-mail from Rachel a few days later. Her pair of cardinals had come. She said that she felt an instant feeling of peace and calm when she spotted them, as she realized that it was her parents, offering love and support. To this day, I still receive periodic e-mails from Rachel. She reports that her cardinals visit regularly and that she feels so very close to her parents. She also states that her life has completely changed, and continues to change, in miraculous ways since she began calling on the angels each and every day.

"I ask them for everything," Rachel says. "They always answer me somehow, and I am grateful."

I had so much fun doing Rachel's reading. Her parents were such a joy to watch as they danced together so eloquently. Rachel had been so distraught for so long, as she felt that she had never connected with her parents before her reading. It always amazes me when loved ones come through with specific signs of how they will be connecting with the ones they've left behind. Rachel's parents told her they would be coming as a pair of cardinals. She listened and believed that it was possible, and she now receives regular visits from them. Once Rachel realized that her parents were still watching over her and began calling on her angels for help, her life changed in miraculous ways. I love it!

Chapter 23

The Blue Dress

I did a reading for a young lady in her early- to midtwenties. As always, I knew nothing of her except her first name and her phone number. As I sat down with Jasmine, I explained how the reading would take place and what to expect. I told her that I was able to connect with loved ones who had passed, as well as angels, guides, and even pets, and that my intention was that she receive whatever she needed the most for healing and moving forward.

I began with my opening prayer, calling in all of our beings of light. Jasmine's father didn't waste any time coming in and began to provide messages for his daughter to help her with her healing. He proceeded to give me specific details of his passing, including the events that led to his demise.

"Oh, my gosh, your dad's car was broadsided," I said. Jasmine's eyes grew big as she nodded yes. I told Jasmine that I often see things in my head like a movie.

"I just want to let you know that I'm actually watching the event happen," I told her. "Your dad's car was broadsided by a large truck, but your dad was standing away from the accident, watching it happen."

Jasmine looked a bit confused, so I continued with what I was seeing in my mind.

"Your dad was lifted out of his car by two guardian angels and was standing with one on either side of him," I said. "They took him out right before impact. They spared him any pain or trauma. He literally

113

watched the whole thing happen from the side of the road. He felt no pain and watched in astonishment as his vehicle was mangled."

Tears rolled down Jasmine's cheeks as she recalled the moments that led to her father's passing. The picture in my head began to shift.

"Now I hear beeping, like machines in a hospital room," I said.

"Those machines have haunted me every day of my life," Jasmine replied.

I began to see Jasmine's father lying in a hospital bed with machines attached to him and told Jasmine what I was witnessing. Then the movie shifted once again. Jasmine's father began to show me a picture of a little girl. I believed it to be Jasmine and began to describe what I was seeing.

"I think he's showing me a picture of you," I told her. "You're about three or four years old, and your dad is holding your hands and twirling you in circles," I continued. "He loves you so much. I can hear the both of you laughing," I began to describe the dress that the little girl was wearing and even drew a picture of it on my notepad. "You have a white and royal-blue dress on. It has a collar that's made from lace or some sort of eyelet material," I continued.

Jasmine didn't recall the dress, so I encouraged her to look through old photos she might have. "I know he's showing me this for a reason," I said. "You must've had a dress like that."

I heard from Jasmine the next day. She had found the picture. The subject line of her e-mail simply said, "Here's the blue dress that you described and drew." Attached to the e-mail was an adorable picture of two little girls in white and royal-blue dresses, exactly how I had described them. They even had the square, lace collar that I had so intricately drawn. Although I am still floored at how amazingly clear loved ones can come through with information, I knew that that little blue dress meant so much more to Jasmine. She had lost her father so many years before, but he was letting her know that he had never left her side. Although he was in heaven, he would continue to love her and guide her as she found her place in the world.

Chapter 24

The Soccer Star

I did a reading for a mother and daughter who had come to connect with several loved ones on the other side. So many loved ones came through, offering their love and support to the two of them. During the reading, a young man came through. I told the women his name and said that he was playing soccer.

"He's kicking a soccer ball around," I said, "and I get is that he's pretty good."

The woman seemed surprised, as this young man was actually the son of a close friend of hers. I told her that her just being there for a reading opened the door to anyone coming in.

"I guess he just wanted to come to let his mother know he was all right," I said. I told the woman that it wasn't her job to call the boy's mother and not to feel any pressure.

"This happens from time to time, and I just don't want you to feel like you're supposed to do anything. It's completely up to you whether or not you contact his mother, and whatever you decide is perfectly fine."

This sort of thing doesn't happen often, but it does happen from time to time. I just feel that it is departed loved ones trying to reach their family however they can. This young man saw an opening to reach his family, and I'm certain that's why he peeked into this particular reading.

The next day, as I was walking my two little dogs along the riverbank that backs up to my house, I came across something quite remarkable. I walked this path daily and had done so for the past five years and knew just about every inch of it. Well, this particular day would be a bit different. As I walked down the path and reached a nearby park, I saw something that stopped me dead in my tracks. There was a big trailer parked in the parking lot of the park with a big banner draped over it. I couldn't believe my eyes as I saw the young man's name that I had mentioned in the reading just the night before. His name was written in big, graffiti letters, and there was a soccer ball next to it. I was floored! I instantly felt the young man right there with me. He was so excited that I had noticed his name, and he was eager to connect with his family.

"Well, I don't usually do this," I told him, "but I will call the woman I spoke with last night and tell her what happened today."

The young man smiled at me and thanked me for helping him. I knew how desperately he wanted to connect with his family and I promised that I would help in whatever way I could. When I got home, I called the woman whom I had spoken with the night before.

"I just had to call you and tell you what happened today, as I really feel he is really trying to let his mother know he is okay."

The woman listened to my story and said that she had already talked with the young man's mother the night before, following her reading. She said she would pass on the information and thanked me for reaching out to her. I did end up meeting the young man's mother. She validated that he had been an excellent soccer player and that after his passing, a scholarship had been set up in his name. That was what the banner was all about, and it was hanging proudly at the soccer field just down the path from my home. I walk by that park often, and during soccer games, I can see this beautiful soul helping all of the young players on the field. Although he is no longer here on a physical level, his spirit lives on in the hearts of those who love the game as much as he did.

Chapter 25

Karisa and the Unicorn

I had the privilege of connecting with a beautiful, young girl named Karisa, who had passed away in terrible house fire. Her mother, Jenny, contacted me for a reading and asked that I see her as soon as possible. I didn't know what Jenny was in need of when she booked her appointment, only that it was important that I see her as soon as I possibly could.

When Jenny arrived for her reading, she looked pale and completely heartbroken. I could feel the pain and anguish she carried in her heart as soon as I greeted her at the door. I had done thousands of readings in the past and had been exposed to so much heartbreak, but Jenny had one of the heaviest hearts I had ever encountered. As we settled in for her reading, I explained that I would be opening with a prayer, calling in all of her angels, guides, and any loved ones who could help. I knew nothing about Jenny other than her first name and phone number and had absolutely no idea that this reading would be one of the most amazing and life-changing readings I would ever do—not only life-changing for my client but for me as well.

I said a prayer and began connecting with Jenny's loved ones and guides. Jenny's daughter, Karisa, came dancing in immediately. I felt such a loving spirit and immediately connected with Karisa's beautiful smile. As Karisa came in, I realized that I had left some music playing and got up to turn it off. I often have beautiful music playing in my home when clients arrive and turn it off before their reading begins. I had forgotten to turn it off this time, until we had already begun. As I stood up to turn the music off, I heard Karisa tell me no.

"She doesn't want me to turn the music off," I told Jenny. "She likes it."

Jenny nodded her head and said that Karisa liked the particular music I was playing and listened to it often when she was alive.

Karisa came through with so many messages for her mother. It was just amazing how crystal clear she was. She was so delightful and had so many loving messages for her mother as well as her father, who, unbeknownst to me, was sitting outside in the car. As Karisa continued to offer messages for both her mother and her father, Jenny asked if she could go and get her husband so that he could hear everything she had to say. I gladly agreed, as Karisa was obviously reaching out to both of them.

After a few moments, Jenny returned with Karisa's father. Messages just started pouring in about hanging out with her father in the garage, riding his motorcycle, and even reminiscing about the pink do-rag she often wore. Karisa's father was overwhelmed. He wiped tears from his eyes as he stared forward, peering out of picture windows that stood on my back deck.

"She wore that pink do-rag all the time," he said.

As Karisa's father continued peering forward, a flock of butterflies suddenly flew by the large picture window straight ahead. I didn't actually see them for myself, but Karisa's father said, "Oh, my God" as he described what he had just witnessed. He proceeded to tell me that one of Karisa's signs was a butterfly and that she often visited both of them that way. We all sat quietly for a few moments, processing what had just happened. We all knew that Karisa had sent that flock of butterflies at that very moment for her father to see.

As the reading continued, I noticed Karisa's parents beginning to shift out of their despair; however, I felt there was something that was still weighing on Jenny's mind. She still looked a bit troubled, as if something hadn't been answered. I looked at Jenny and asked, "Is there anything else you needed to know today?"

Jenny began to tell me that she felt as though Karisa's death was all her fault. She explained that on the night of the fire, she was holding Karisa's hand in hers as they were trying to escape down the stairs from the second floor, where they had been sleeping. They were approximately halfway down the stairs when she realized that Karisa's hand was gone.

"I couldn't believe it," she said. "One minute, we were running down the stairs hand in hand, and then she was gone."

Jenny lost her somehow and couldn't find her, as the smoke had gotten so thick. Jenny described how that picture had played over and over in her head and how she couldn't get rid of it.

"It haunts me every single day," Jenny said. "I just need to know what happened to Karisa."

As I focused on Jenny's question, visions of what had happened began to pour in. I shared what I saw as it began to unfold within my mind. I saw all of the smoke around Karisa and her mother. It was thick and dark, making it difficult to see anything. I could hear them coughing and watched as they made their way down the stairs. I saw Karisa's hand slip out from her mother's, and as it happened, two angels lifted her up and out of the smoke. Although I saw the angels lift Karisa's body completely out of the fire-ravaged home, I knew that it was actually her soul that they had lifted up and out.

"The angels placed her on top of a unicorn," I said. I continued telling Karisa's parents that I saw the unicorn take her up and away from the fire.

"She wasn't scared and didn't feel anything," I told them. "The angels and that unicorn spared her any fear or pain."

As I finished telling Karisa's parents what I was seeing, I told them that I had never seen a unicorn in a reading before.

"Oh, I believe they exist," I told them, "but I've never connected with one like that before while giving a reading."

As the reading came to an end, Karisa's parents seemed more at peace. Of course, nothing would ever be able to replace their beloved daughter, but they were relieved that the angels had taken care of Karisa and that she didn't suffer. Their reading came to an end and we hugged one another and said our good-byes. As I watched Karisa's parents walk down the steps from my porch, I could see little Karisa skipping alongside of them. Oh, how I wished they could sense their daughter beside them! I didn't know if I would ever talk with Karisa's parents again, but I felt so much love coming from this beautiful young girl who died so young. I felt blessed to have connected with such a beautiful soul and asked the angels to help Karisa's parents continue with their healing.

I heard from Jenny a couple of weeks later. She called and left a message on my phone and stated that she had something amazing to tell me. I called back as soon as I could, as I was eager to hear what she had to say. Jenny answered the phone and told me that she had told her neighbors all about the reading she had had with me. She said she had told them everything, even the part about the angels placing Karisa on top of a unicorn.

"I didn't care how crazy I sounded," Jenny said. "I just had to tell them." Jenny continued and told me that her neighbors were stunned when she mentioned the unicorn. "They just stared at me with their mouths open," she said.

It turns out that Jenny's neighbors had taken pictures of the house that evening as it was engulfed in flames. When they were looking at the pictures later, they were taken aback by the clouds of smoke that rose above the house, as they were in the shape of a horse. As you can imagine, I was completely shocked and surprised at what I was hearing.

"Oh, my gosh!" I exclaimed. "The angels really did place her on that unicorn."

I went silent, and tears welled up in my eyes as I tried to process what I was hearing. After a big, silent pause, I said, quite simply, "Well, I guess unicorns really do exist."

Jenny and I chuckled in amazement. This was just the validation Karisa's parents needed. The angels had stepped in and helped Karisa, placing her on her special unicorn. She had been spared any pain or trauma and had been whisked away to heaven. She was riding her unicorn all over heaven's green, rolling hills and was spreading love and light everywhere she went.

Chapter 26

Aunt Betty

I did a reading for a colleague of mine. She was an occupational therapist and worked in the same county that I had worked in providing early-intervention services. Susan had contacted me on several occasions, always expressing an interest in "setting up something soon," but she had some reluctance when it came to scheduling an actual date. I understood Susan's hesitation, as she had been brought up to believe that what I did might be something evil. Each time we talked, I could feel Susan's deep desire to book a reading, but it would take months for her to finally do it. I asked the angels to help her with her decision, and she finally took the plunge. Susan booked a reading for herself and her mother. They were coming together, and, according to Susan, they were both eager and very nervous.

When Susan and her mother arrived, I immediately felt very anxious and tense. I knew that I was feeling their emotions and quickly reassured them that I only got "good stuff."

They giggled nervously as one of them replied, "That's good."

I opened with a prayer calling in all of our angels and guides and dove right in. Loved ones began coming in immediately.

"There are so many waiting to speak with you," I told Susan and her mother. There were parents, grandparents, siblings, cousins, you name it! I was amazed at the number of people that came forward. They knew a lot of people in heaven, that's for sure. After a significant amount of time had passed and we had connected with several different loved ones, each offering his or her first name upon entering the reading, I paused and asked if there was anyone else they wanted to connect with that hadn't come through yet. They both replied yes and gave me the name Betty. Betty showed up as soon as I said her name. I felt so much love coming from her, and she couldn't wait to connect with "two of her favorite people in the whole world."

Susan and her mother began to weep as Betty came through. She was a little ball of energy and had so much to say. Betty brought up so many memories and spoke in such detail. Susan and her mother could hardly contain themselves as they listened to the words come out of my mouth.

"Betty watches over your little girl," I told Susan. "She says that she plays with her every single day."

Susan sobbed as she said, "My daughter tells me that Aunt Betty is with her every day, playing in her room. I just wasn't sure until now."

I saw a gentleman playing with Susan's daughter as well and gave Susan his name as well as a description.

"It's my grandfather," she answered. Susan seemed a little confused and stated that her grandfather had never met her daughter.

"That doesn't matter," I quickly answered. "Your loved ones, even those whom you never knew, will act as guides for you and your children." Sadie was his great-granddaughter, and he was going to help her and guide her as much as he could. Susan seemed relieved at knowing that there were several people watching over her precious daughter. She had always wondered if Aunt Betty was around her daughter as her daughter had said, but she had no idea that her grandfather was watching over her as well.

Aunt Betty continued to come through with amazing and loving messages for the rest of the reading. At one point, I saw a big bouquet of sunflowers. I looked at Susan and said, "Your aunt comes as sunflowers."

Susan burst into tears once again. She told me that her neighbor had just given her a bouquet of sunflowers the week before, for no apparent reason.

"Wow," I said. "You just can't make this stuff up!" The three of us just sat there laughing for quite some time.

At the end of the reading, I asked Susan to turn her cards over. I often have clients pick three cards from one of my many angel card decks at the beginning of the reading, instructing them that we will look at the cards at the end of the reading. Loved ones, angels, and guides often come through with validation of messages I've provided for my client during the reading, or they may provide additional messages that make sense for their loved ones left behind.

"Betty is so excited and can hardly wait for you to turn your cards over," I told Susan. As Susan turned the first card over, she let out a big cry. The card was that of an angel with her arms spread wide that read "debt-free." It was apparent that Susan was in complete shock at what she was seeing. She told me that Betty's last instruction at the time of her passing was to completely pay off all of Susan's college debt and the family had honored her wishes. The three of us sat there speechless for a few moments as we tried to wrap our heads around what had just happened. I remember that although the room was filled with complete silence, you could feel the overwhelming love that Betty held in her heart for these two amazing women. I thanked Betty for coming in so clearly and for giving Susan and her mother the closure they needed to receive. I sent Susan and her mother on their way and asked the angels to continue with the healing that had begun that day.

I received an e-mail from Susan that evening. She told me that when she got home, she decided to ask her daughter if her great-grandpa ever came to play with her. Her daughter had always talked about Aunt Betty being there but never mentioned anyone else. When she asked Sadie if her great-grandfather ever came to play, she said, "Yes, he comes every day."

Susan thanked me over and over and told me that things would never be the same.

"This has changed my life, Julia. I can't thank you enough."

I could feel Susan's gratitude inside my soul, and I knew she was on her way to amazing and magical things. She had resisted coming for a reading for so long because of what she was taught to believe. Fear had been running the show for so very long. Now she had her own beliefs, beliefs that she could honor, beliefs that made sense for her.

Chapter 27

Kate's Imaginary Friends

Over the years, I've met many unique and amazing children while working as a speech pathologist. I have always focused on each child's unique gifts and abilities, never on his or her disability. I always felt it a big part of my mission to help parents see all of their child's amazing abilities and help them believe in infinite possibilities, rather than falling into the beliefs that their child was somehow broken and would never reach his or her true potential. I gained the trust of many parents and had a special bond with so many of the children I saw. I felt so much love for them and knew that they felt the same for me.

Many of the children who have come across my path have had the gift of sensing spirit, and parents would often speak about their child's "imaginary friends." I was pretty good at knowing which parents were open to what might really be going on and was careful about which ones I approached about the subject. Nonetheless, whether or not I felt that the parents were open or not, I would always suggest that they encourage their children to play with these friends, as it was helping them tap into their imagination. I knew that some of them were actually having conversations with deceased loved ones, angels and guides, but like I said, that's not something every parent is eager to hear. One little girl in particular comes to mind. Kate had an amazing connection, and I was in awe of her abilities. Although she was only two years old at the time, she was definitely an old soul. Kate knew things and said things that just don't normally come out of a two-year-old's mouth. Her mother was quite aware of her uniqueness and often wondered if there was more going on in that tiny little head than she could ever imagine.

Little Kate warmed up to me quickly and we became close friends in no time. Kate's mother was both surprised and impressed with how quickly Kate warmed up to me. She told me that she generally acted shy with adults, but I guess she just looked at me as a big kid who came to play with her once a week. Kate was a bit behind in her expressive-language skills and although it was considered to be a significant delay at the time, I knew Kate would make big strides in no time. She was eager to play and learn and would do just about anything I asked of her. As Kate's mother and I got to know each other, we became quite close.

During one of my visits, Kate's mother began telling me that Kate often walked around the house talking to her imaginary friends. She said that she would have long, drawn-out conversations with them and that it really appeared as if she was talking to someone. Kate's mother finally confided in me one day.

"You might think I'm crazy, but I think Kate might be talking to some of my family members." I was tickled to death to hear Kate's mother utter those words, as I had always felt that Kate had the ability to connect with the spirit world.

"Oh, my gosh," I said. "Do you have any idea what else I do?"

Kate's mother looked puzzled as she replied no.

"I am an medium, and I have the ability to connect with angels and people who have passed," I answered.

Kate's mother looked astonished at what I had just told her, and we both just starting laughing.

"I don't think you're crazy," I said. "I think you're right on. I believe Kate has the ability to sense spirit around her."

Kate's mother looked relieved that someone believed her. I'm sure it wasn't easy deciding to come out about her daughter's special abilities with her daughter's speech therapist, but I'm thrilled that she felt comfortable enough to do so. I told Kate's mom that I had felt for quite some time that Kate was talking with deceased family members and guides but didn't know how to bring it up in conversation. *Whew,*

I thought. The cat was out of the bag, and now we could talk openly about just how amazing little Kate was.

Kate was so sensitive, even to sounds, tastes, textures, and energy in general. I had always been concerned that Kate would receive a diagnosis of Asperger's syndrome or autism because she was a little quirky. Kate was just different, that's all, and she was a young person with amazing intuitive abilities. Kate's mother and I talked for so long that day. She had so many questions about her daughter's abilities and was eager to learn the best way to help her.

"Do you know who Kate is talking to?" she asked.

"Yes," I said. "She talks with an older couple. They are husband and wife. I believe they are your aunt and uncle. They sit at the dining room table sometimes and drink coffee." I walked over and pointed to the chairs where I saw the two sitting as I gave her the two names I was hearing.

"Oh, my God!" she exclaimed. "That's where my aunt and uncle always sat. This is their house. And those are their names." She let out a nervous giggle, and I quickly put her at ease.

"They're not still here like ghosts or anything like that," I told her. "They come and go and are two of Kate's guides. They watch over her, as they know just how special she is. They help her."

Kate's mother paused for a moment and then said, "But they never knew her."

I explained that loved ones often act as guides, for us and for our children, and they can even act as guides for generations to come.

"They were in your family line," I told her. "They will help anyone who needs them." Kate's mother seemed relieved as I told her that her aunt and uncle had been with Kate since birth. "They will never leave her side," I assured her.

Kate's mother and I would talk many more times. She was fascinated with Kate's abilities and seemed to be notice so much more after our initial conversation.

"I feel that there is someone else Kate talks to," she said one day.

"Oh, there are several," I replied. I assured her that they were all beings of light and that they were all helping Kate.

"I even see Archangel Michael," I said. "He comes and talks to Kate and teaches her things. He said she's bossy."

We both started laughing hysterically. Kate was known to be a bit bossy to her siblings and even her imaginary friends. She was always telling them what to do and how to do it.

"I know it must be difficult sometimes, but try not to be scared or nervous about Kate's abilities. She is here to do amazing things. She is here to share her light with the world," I told her mom.

Kate's mother again looked relieved, as she was beginning to realize that her daughter was an amazing light.

"I just can't wait to see what she does," she said proudly.

Over the next few months, Kate's mother became more and more relaxed. Although she had been brought up Catholic and was taught that what was happening with her daughter was something "evil" or "dark," she said she felt such a sense of calmness about the whole thing.

"I only feel love when Kate is talking to my aunt and uncle," she told me. "I can feel them with her and know that they are guiding her on her journey." Kate's mother followed one of the suggestions I had given her early on. She posted pictures of her aunt and uncle where her daughter could see them. She said that Kate waves at the pictures every time she passes by and often stops and talks to them.

"It was funny," she said. "When I put the pictures up initially, Kate walked by and said, 'Oh, hi!'"

It was such an amazing experience to watch Kate as she connected with some of her guides, her great-aunt and -uncle. It was even more amazing to watch her mother accept and embrace Kate's gift. I can't wait to see what becomes of Kate. I know she is destined to do amazing things!

Now on to a story about a beautiful little boy who had the ability to see baby angels ...

Chapter 28

The Cherubs

I received a referral for a little boy in a nearby town. He was born with multiple issues, and I was one of several therapists who had been assigned to see him. He was born with significant delays in all areas of development and would have a difficult road ahead, but I had seen miracles happen before and I knew that there were unlimited possibilities just waiting for him and his family. Joey was truly a miracle, and honestly, one of the most beautiful little boys I had ever met. He had such an amazing smile, beautiful, twinkling eyes, and an amazing spirit. There was something about him that I just couldn't put my finger on. I knew he was special, and I knew he was here for a reason.

I saw Joey weekly for speech and feeding therapy. We had so much fun playing with toys and trying new foods. We bonded quickly, and I treasured our time together. In no time, I began to notice Joey doing something odd during our sessions. During our sessions together, Joey would often seem like he was looking right above my head. He would stare and start giggling, and his mother and I noticed it was happening at just about every session. He would stare over my head, giggling and kicking his arms and legs in excitement. His mother and I couldn't help but laugh along, and we often wondered what he was seeing. I wondered if there was an angel that stood behind me or perhaps one of Joey's loved ones who were making him laugh, but, of course, I kept that to myself. I could recall a handful of children who had done the same thing. It didn't seem to dawn on me that they were all seeing something over my

128

head until Joey began to do it so frequently. My curiosity was piqued, to say the least.

A few months later, while I was getting a reading from my mentor, she paused for a moment and asked, "Do children often look over your head?"

The question surely would have sounded strange to anyone else, but I knew exactly what she was talking about.

"Yes," I replied. "It happens quite often, as a matter of fact."

After a brief pause, she answered, "They see cherubs. There are little baby angels that fly over your head. The children see them." Wow! I couldn't believe it! I had cherubs around me and the kids could see them? How cool was that! I'll have to admit, I didn't know much about cherubs at the time and had only seen pictures of them in stores or catalogs that sold such items. My mentor continued and told me that these cherubs are with me all the time and that they are helping me with the children I work with.

"Ah, that explains a lot," I said. "Now I know what the children are seeing. That is so cool!" No wonder all of those children were smiling and giggling so much as they looked over my head. Those little cherubs must be putting on quite a show for them. I felt such joy come over me in knowing that the cherubs had stepped forward to help me on my path. I knew that I was doing something good, and it just felt right.

Here is another story about cherubs involving one of my clients. It happened a couple of years after I was told about the cherubs who flew over my head. It turns out I'm not the only one who has them flying over me.

A few years after I had learned about the cherubs, I had the honor of doing a reading for a young man who received frequent visits from these sweet little angels as well. John had come to see me in hopes of connecting with his father. He had many regrets and so much had been left unsaid between the two of them, and he longed to just know that his father wasn't upset with him. John's father came through with clear and concise messages. There was such urgency about his message, as he was desperate to let his son know that he loved him.

"Your dad says that he doesn't hold any anger or blame about anything. He only wants you to be happy," I told him. John's eyes filled with tears as he listened to his father's words. "He keeps showing me a model train and a bunch of watches."

John said that he had his father's model train set and his collection of watches and had been given them after his passing.

"They mean so much to me," John said as he acknowledged his father's approval that they were in the right spot.

"Your dad said that you have a new baby boy," I said.

John's face lit up as he quickly replied, "Yes."

"Your dad says that he knew your son even before you did. He took care of him in heaven until it was time for him to come." John's eyes filled with tears once again and he began to cry.

"I always wished my dad could've met my son," he said, to which I replied, "Well, now you know he did."

As the reading progressed, I told John that I could see his son smiling and giggling. "He's such a beautiful little boy. Oh, my gosh, he looks over your head sometimes, right?" I asked this as I was seeing it happen, like a movie in my head.

"Yes, he does it a lot," John replied.

"He sees cherubs," I told him as I began to literally see them dance over John's head right there in my dining room. "There are so many!"

Just then, John's father spoke up and said that his little boy also saw him from time to time.

"Your dad wants you to know that your son sees him sometimes too and that he recognizes him from the time they were in heaven together." It was clear that John was overwhelmed with emotion. He was crying, but they were clearly tears of joy. "Your dad says that the worst is now behind you. Your baby boy is here to help you heal."

John shook his head in amazement. He proceeded to tell me that he had lived a life of addiction, guilt, and shame, until his little boy came into his life.

"I don't know what happened," John said. "When my son was born, I just decided I was going to turn myself around."

"Well, your father is very proud of you," I told him. "He says that you've become the man he always knew you could be."

As John's reading came to an end, I walked him to the front door. It was so funny at the time. Here was this big, grown man, shaking his head and laughing, and all he could say was, "So there's little cherubs flying over my head!" It was priceless.

Now I'm going to shift gears and talk about a wonderful experience I had with some amazing horses. What happened at Phoenix Rizing Stables would change my life forever.

Chapter 29

The Healing Horses of Phoenix Rizing Stables

I had the most amazing experience while working with a horse named Sam. I received a call from a friend who had taken him in as a boarder at her stables. Corey and her mother Dorothy are owners of Phoenix Rizing Stables in Harvey's Lake, Pennsylvania, and they had taken Sam in about two weeks before calling me. When I received the call from Corey, she said that she had a horse that needed some help. Sam had shown up to her ranch very underweight. He had no energy and his health seemed to be continuing to decline at a very rapid pace. Corey and her mother had been to me for readings and were aware that I also did healing work, and they were desperate to figure out how to help Sam.

"Would you mind coming out and taking a look at him? Maybe you can get something about what's going on with him," she asked.

At the time, I was mentoring a group of teenagers and had attuned them all to Reiki, and I knew this would be a perfect place for them to practice their skills. I quickly agreed and scheduled a time for the kids and I to drive out to Corey's place the following weekend.

When we arrived at the stables, Corey walked us into the barn. She began to fill us in on Sam's condition and warned us that it was bad. As you might recall, Sam was only a boarder at Phoenix Rizing Stables. His owner paid Corey to feed and care for him. Corey explained that she had talked with Sam's owner on several occasions and expressed her concern about his condition and that he continued to decline, but his owner would not take any action. We didn't know at the time, but Sam had been diagnosed with Lyme disease, a very debilitating disease that is quite expensive to treat in horses.

"He's really bad," Corey told me. "I just want you to be prepared for what you're going to see."

The kids and I waited in the barn as Corey went out to the field to get Sam. I remember calling all of my angels in to surround us at that moment and asking them to guide me. *Please guide me and show me what to do*, I remember saying quietly in my head. I knew that the angels were with us, and I was confident that we could help Sam somehow.

"Just tune into your abilities as healers," I told the kids. "You'll know what to do."

A few minutes later, Corey entered the barn with Sam in tow. He was wearing a nice blanket, as it was late fall and was getting a bit chilly outside. Corey walked him to the middle of the stables, tied him to a post, and gently removed his blanket. As I looked at Sam, my heart began to break. He was emaciated and appeared to be quite weak. Instead of holding his head upright and high like most horses, Sam's hung low. His eyes were dull, and my heart went out to this broken-down shell of a horse standing in front of me. The kids and I began talking to Sam and stroking his coat. I was amazed at the children as they began working on Sam. One was giving him Reiki as she stroked his head, in the area of his crown chakra and third eye. Another was gently brushing him as she whispered loving messages. One of the boys in the group kneeled down, closed his eyes, and began giving Reiki to Sam's knees. I was in awe. They were following their inner guidance and knew exactly what to do.

As I began to lay my hands on Sam, asking for any guidance, I became overwhelmed with emotion.

"He has no spirit," I said as tears came to my eyes. "He has no purpose. He has no will to live because he has no purpose," I continued. "He feels like he's been thrown away."

Tears began to flow as I felt Sam's anguish. I stepped away and walked into a nearby room, trying to get myself together. Corey came into the office to see if I was okay.

"I don't want the kids to see me this upset," I told her. I regained my composure after a few minutes and headed back out to where Sam was standing. I put my hands on Sam once again and began infusing him with healing energy. As I moved around his body, stopping where I felt guided to, I noticed something unusual on his neck. I called Corey over to take a look at what I had discovered.

"Sam has an infinity symbol on his neck," I said while pointing to what I had found.

"Oh, my gosh," she replied. "He sure does." Corey assured me that it wasn't a branding mark and walked me toward his back end to show me where his brand had been placed on his hindquarters.

"That is crazy," I said as I walked back up to take a look at the symbol on his neck once again. "This is a sign that something amazing is going to happen. I just know it."

Although I had no idea what it all meant just yet, I knew that there were things happening behind the scenes that we would all become aware of, when it was time for them to be revealed to us.

The kids were having a ball with Sam and had even braided his tail, and you could feel all of the love they were pouring into him. John, the one who had been giving Reiki to Sam's knees, looked up at me and said, "I think it's done," indicating that Sam had received the Reiki he needed that day.

I told Corey that we would come back to work on Sam again very soon. I wasn't sure when, but I felt that I would be guided as to what to do next. I said a closing prayer, asking the angels to watch over Sam and help him with his healing. We said our good-byes and the children and I headed home.

The ride home was such a delight. The kids talked about their experience with Sam, sharing things that had happened while they worked on him. They were amazed at how they knew where to put their hands. I told them how proud I was of them and that they had done such an amazing job tuning in to their own inner guidance. They all seemed proud of themselves, but more importantly, they realized that they had just done something truly amazing. They were healers and knew what it felt like to tap into their innate healing abilities and they couldn't wait to do it again.

As I returned home, I just couldn't seem to get Sam off my mind. I thought about him constantly and continued to ask my angels and guides for any guidance. One day, as I was meditating, I got my message. I was to attune Sam to Reiki.

"What?" I asked, as I had no idea how I was supposed to do that.

"You will know what to do," was their response.

I called Corey and scheduled to go see Sam the following weekend. "I'm coming by myself," I told her. "I'm supposed to do this alone this time. I will be attuning Sam to Reiki."

As the next few days went by, I began to receive visions of how I was to attune Sam to Reiki. I saw myself working in the area of his head and his back. "Horses heal by way of their back," is what I heard inside of my head. *Hmm,* I thought. *That makes sense.* I had a plan, and I was eager to carry it out.

Saturday rolled around, and I found myself both excited and nervous as I headed to Phoenix Rizing Stables once again. I wasn't sure why I felt so nervous but I knew deep down that something big was going to happen. As I prepared for the drive, which was about forty-five minutes from my home, I was guided to take a gift for Sam. I had a few feathers that I had had bound in leather and beads. I was to take it to Sam and hang it on his halter. Although I didn't know exactly who was telling me to do this, I knew that there were Native Americans helping Sam with his healing. I had seen them drumming on Corey's land before, and I knew they were a powerful bunch. The feathers would be their symbol that they were watching over him. I found out later on that many Native Americans had traveled over the land where Sam was being boarded. I wasn't surprised that they wanted to help with the healing of this beautiful animal.

As I drove the forty-five minutes from my home to the stables, I continued to receive guidance as to what I was supposed to do once I got there. I was to attune all of the horses, not just Sam, as they would now be known as "The Healing Horses of Phoenix Rizing Stables." I can't begin to describe what was going on inside of me. I was so excited at hearing this that I actually had to pull over and walk around a bit to get grounded. I couldn't wait to tell Corey that I was going to attune all of her horses. I knew she would be so thrilled, as she often worked with children with disabilities, teaching them to ride. This made so much sense to me. The horses of Phoenix Rizing Stables would be healing the children and adults who rode them in more ways than one.

Corey and her mother, Dorothy, greeted me when I arrived. I told them what I had been guided to do and that I wanted to attune all of the horses. "It will not only benefit the horses, but will also benefit anyone who rides them," I explained.

They were thrilled and couldn't wait to get started. We decided that the best way for me to attune each horse was to bring them into the barn individually. Corey and Dorothy would bring each horse in one by one, where they would receive their attunement. Then they would be led out to the pasture, bringing the next horse in with them when they returned. Corey walked into the barn with the first horse to be attuned, Jazz. Jazz had taken a liking to Sam and had stepped in as sort of an overseer. He always had to know where Sam was, and from what I was told, the feelings were mutual for Sam. Corey tied Jazz up and she and her mother headed into the office, as they wanted to give me some privacy as I attuned the horses.

The attunements went smoothly and easily. It was a beautiful experience, and I knew exactly what to do, just as I had been guided I would. I felt so connected to each and every one of the horses as I attuned them with the Reiki symbols. They stood calmly and quietly, without moving at all, as if they knew what was happening. At the beginning of the attunements, each of them looked back in my direction as if to say, "I am ready." It was obvious that they were very willing participants, as they accepted the attunements in such a calm and gentle manner.

When I had finished with all of the attunements and the last horse had been led back out to the pasture, Corey and Dorothy came into the barn where I was gathering my things. As they approached, they asked an interesting question.

"Did you hear any music during any of the attunements?"

I told them that I hadn't heard any music at all. They proceeded to tell me that they had heard music on two different occasions during the attunements. Corey described it as sounding like "church music." Her mother agreed and said that it sounded like organ music or something you would hear in church, almost angelic. I told them that I didn't hear any music and that it must have been something just for them to hear.

"I guess it was something special, just for you," I told them.

We all smiled and shrugged our shoulders as we finished gathering my things. We agreed that something definitely seemed different.

"There's just something in the air," I said. "It's a good feeling."

Now we would just have to wait and see if anything would change with Sam. I turned to Corey and Dorothy and said, "The healing has begun," as that was the guidance I was receiving at that very moment.

"Sam is a champion," I told them. "He was a champion once before, and he will be a champion again." The words just seemed to flow out of my mouth as I spoke. I knew that this was guidance from above, and I knew that we were to trust that it was so. The messages continued to flow, and I looked at Dorothy and asked, "You know that song 'We Are the Champions?'" She nodded her head yes. "Well, you're supposed to start singing it to Sam." We all chucked a bit at what I was asking her to do. "No, really, sing it to him every day and tell him over and over that he is a champion. The angels say it is very important that you do this."

"I'll do it," Dorothy replied. I had such a peaceful and loving feeling inside as I drove home that evening. I just loved working with the horses that day and knew that I wanted to do more of it. I knew that they had filled me up with as much love and light as I had given to them. I felt at peace, and I had hope in my heart. I knew that there was a miracle coming for Sam, and I couldn't wait for it to unfold.

"Thank you, angels, for helping today. Thank you for guiding me as to what to do and what to say. Thank you for always being there for me," I said as I drove away.

I received a message from Corey the next day. She reminded me of the music that they had heard the day before. "Well," she said, "my grandmother passed away yesterday, and Mom and I figured out that it happened right around the time we heard that music."

I was floored!

"Oh, Corey, I'm so sorry for your loss." I was lost for words for a few moments and then added, "What an amazing gift. You and your mother were able to hear the angels calling your grandmother home."

Corey said that that was exactly what she and her mother had thought when they received the news. We were all amazed at what had happened, and I knew that the angels had helped bring their beloved home. The choirs of angels had sung so loudly that Corey and her mother were able to hear them. And they could rest easy knowing that their beloved mother and grandmother was resting safely in the angels' arms.

Over the next few weeks, I found myself thinking about Sam all of the time. I would pray for him and send him healing energy and ask the angels to watch over him. I felt so connected to him and couldn't help but wonder if we had met before in a past life. I would tear up at the thought of losing Sam and would immediately say, "Cancel, clear, delete," when those thoughts would creep in and replace them with things like, "Thank you for giving Sam a miracle." I would check in with Corey periodically, and she reported that Sam was getting stronger and that he was gaining weight. She was happy to report that he had so much more energy and was beginning to act like a horse again. I grew eager to see Sam's progress and scheduled a time to go and see him once again.

I took one of the kids from Team Halo with me on my trip, John, whom you might remember was the one who was giving Sam Reiki in his knees. I felt it was important for John to see Sam, as he had also expressed feeling such a deep connection with him. We made our way to the ranch and couldn't wait to see our friend once again. As we pulled into the driveway, we noticed all of the horses grazing in the field above the barn. We looked for Sam and were surprised when we realized that he had gained enough weight that he blended in with the other horses.

We both had trouble spotting him at first. Corey and Dorothy greeted us as we got out of the car.

"I can't wait to see Sam," I told them both. Corey asked John if he wanted to go with her to get Sam, and he gladly accepted. I waited eagerly in the barn with Dorothy. After a few minutes, John walked into the barn with Sam. He was beautiful! He had filled out and his coat was full and shiny, far from the emaciated body and dull coat he wore just a few weeks before. I walked over and touched Sam's forehead. We locked eyes and I could feel his gratitude.

"His spirit is back," I told Corey as tears welled up in my eyes. I had no idea why I felt so connected to this horse, but I knew that we had met before. I loved him so much, and I knew the feeling was mutual.

John and I enjoyed our time with Sam. We brushed him and gave him treats. Corey told me that someone was coming to look at Sam that weekend, someone who might be interested in adopting him. As Corey spoke, that movie that often plays in my head began to roll.

"There's a young girl that is looking for Sam," I said. "Sam belongs with her. They're supposed to be together."

Corey looked at me with hopeful eyes. She wanted desperately to find him a wonderful home and out of the hands of his current owner, who had tried to sell him when he was so sick. Dorothy motioned with her arm and called me over to Sam's stall.

"I just have to show you something," she said. Dorothy was pointing at a small piece of paper that was tacked up on Sam's stall door. It read, "Be the champion you were meant to be."

"That's the song you told me to sing to Sam, remember?" she asked.

"Yes, I remember," I replied.

"Well, I sing that song to him every single day. One evening, Corey and I went out for dinner, and this was in my fortune cookie."

"Oh, my God!" I said as I giggled. "Talk about getting validation!"

We smiled at each other, as we knew deep down that there was something magical going on with Sam. We knew that there was something—or someone—bigger than us working on his behalf, and we knew that he was going to be okay.

As John and I got ready to leave, I looked at Corey and Dorothy and told them that the love they had given to Sam had helped him heal.

"You are both so amazing," I said. "You have no idea how happy the angels are. You saved this precious soul, and they will be forever grateful for your love and generosity." As John and I got in the car, I turned to Corey and her mother and said, "The girl who is coming for Sam will love him unconditionally. They are meant to be together, and the angels are arranging everything." Corey and her mother both grinned from ear to ear, as they knew in their hearts that what I was saying was true.

Over the next couple of weeks, I prayed and prayed that Sam's new owner would find him easily. It didn't take long before I received a phone call from Corey.

"Sam is being adopted," she told me. "The young girl you told us about came to see him and fell in love with him instantly."

I'll have to admit, I was extremely happy that Sam had found his new owner, but I was also very sad. I knew that I would have to say good-bye to Sam, and that was not going to be easy. Over those very short few months, I had grown quite attached to him.

"I'm so happy," I managed to say while choking back tears. Corey continued and told me that Sam had taken to the young girl immediately as well. "It's as if they've always been together," she said. As desperately as I tried, I couldn't fight back the tears.

"It'll be hard to see him go," I told her, "but I know he's going to be with whom he is supposed to be." After we hung up, I asked the angels, and in particular, Archangel Michael, to help me cut any cords to Sam.

"Thank you for helping him get to his perfect home," I prayed. "Now help me let go of him so we can both move forward."

I went to see Sam one last time before he went to his new home. It had been several weeks since I had seen him, and I had no idea what to expect. As I drove up to the barn, I looked around at all of the horses. I couldn't figure out which one he was. This had been easy in the past, as he had been "the skinny one" with patches of hair missing throughout his coat. As I reached the top of the drive and pulled in next to the barn, one of the horses looked up and turned in my direction. It was Sam. He was absolutely stunning, his coat so shiny and smooth. He was no longer thin and was full of defined muscles. He stood tall and proud, just like all of the other horses. Tears began to flow down my cheeks; I felt so much love for him. I was so proud of him. He had become the champion that I knew he was. Corey brought Sam over to the barn, where I was standing. I couldn't get over how amazing he looked. He had a confidence and cockiness about him that I had never seen before. It was breathtaking. I stroked his neck a few times and thanked him for the lesson. Sam had taught me so much, but most of all, to never give up. I hugged Sam one last time before Corey put him back in the pasture. As he entered the yard, he turned and looked back at me, as if he was saying "thank you." He turned away and ran faster than I had ever seen, like a racehorse, back to the other horses. Sam had his spirit back. He looked like a champion, and I knew that his future was bright.

"This is not the last of Sam," I told Corey and her mother. "I have a feeling we'll be hearing a lot more about him in the near future."

My ride home proved to be much happier than I thought it would be. I envisioned Sam running in the fields and finally feeling like he fit it with the others. I asked the angels to continue watching over him and asked them to remain with him for as long as he needed them. I thanked God and the angels for Sam's miraculous recovery and found myself feeling full of love and peace.

"Thank you for allowing me to be a witness to this miraculous healing," I prayed. "I will never forget this amazing experience. I am grateful."

Corey contacted me with updates on Sam from time to time. His new owner continued to nurture and love him, and she began to train him. She started entering him in competitions, and Sam really began to shine. To date, Sam has placed and received ribbons in several statewide competitions. Sam became the true champion that I knew he was. He validated that with unconditional love and the angel's help, anything is possible. Thank you, Sam. I will never forget you.

Here's a picture of Sam with some of the kids from Team Halo. He taught us so much and we will forever be grateful. We love you Sam. You will always be a champion to us!

Chapter 30

Nikki – Still Making Wishes Come True

I was invited to do a group reading in a nearby town. There were about ten people present who were all eager to connect with loved ones they had lost. I gave the group some basic instructions and began with an opening prayer. As I began the reading, I was immediately surrounded by one of the most amazing, loving, and enthusiastic little girls I had ever connected with. She bounced in with such joy and love, and I could see her holding something in her hand.

"I see a young girl who is so full of life," I said. "She's holding a wand in her hand with a star on the end."

As I described what I was seeing, a gentleman at the end of the table spoke up and said, "That's my daughter, Nikki."

"Oh, my gosh, I absolutely love her," I said, smiling in his direction. "She is so bubbly, and she just runs around with that wand everywhere." I paused for a moment before continuing. "Nikki's a greeter in heaven. She greets so many children. She uses her wand to make their wishes come true, but she is also using it to help all of you."

Her father, Chuck, laughed a bit and said, "That sounds like her." He went on to tell me that his daughter had been the spokesperson for the Make-A-Wish Foundation while she was living. She had touched so many lives and had left her mark here on earth in such a short time.

"Wow," I exclaimed. "She's carrying on her work in heaven."

As the reading continued, I told Chuck that Nikki was sitting on his lap. "She says that she does this regularly," I told him.

"She does," he replied. "She comes around me all the time, and I can actually feel her sitting with me sometimes."

"She loves you so much," I said. "Nikki is such an old soul. She seems so mature for her age," I told her father.

"She was," Chuck replied. "She was so much older than her chronological age. She helped everyone," he said proudly, "especially all of the kids who were at the hospital with her."

Throughout the evening, Nikki came through with several messages for her father. I felt so drawn to talk with him further to discuss his daughter at length. I just knew that her story would be able to help others, and I was elated when he agreed to share her amazing story. Although Nikki's journey was a difficult one, she always found time to help others. Here's just a little more about this amazing young lady who inspired so many in such a short time.

Nikki was diagnosed with cystic fibrosis at the age of fourteen, and although her prognosis was grim, Nikki's father said that you would never know it if you spent any time with her. Although Nikki's condition was terminal, her spirit never died. Nikki was such a positive person and devoted much of her time to helping others deal with and cope with their own illnesses. She spent countless hours at Saint Christopher's Hospital in Philadelphia, where she received treatment for her disease, but her father says that Nikki would often push her own needs aside to visit other children in the ward, trying to help them cope with what was happening to them. Even though she was so young herself, Nikki mentored many of the other children and helped them accept their fate.

"She would tell them about all of the amazing things that were waiting for them in heaven," Chuck said. "She had a real gift at making them feel better about everything."

Nikki was wise beyond her years and helped many of the children release their fears of dying. To hear Chuck tell the story is priceless. He knows that his daughter's illness actually turned out to be a blessing for so many.

As Nikki's illness progressed, she never stopped trying to help others. She continued to be involved in every telethon, trying desperately to let her voice be heard. Chuck reported that if at any time she needed to go to the hospital for treatment at the same time a telethon was going to happen, she would only go if she could be out in time to attend it. Chuck says that she would show up with her oxygen on and would refuse to leave the event until every wish was granted.

Chuck reports that Nikki visits him often. He says he can actually feel her sit with him on his bed from time to time, particularly when he's down in the dumps. He knows it's Nikki letting him know that she will always be there for him, trying to cheer him up like she always did. Chuck says that Nikki also comes to him through songs. He often hears one of Nikki's favorite songs, which she used to sing around the house, "How Can I Live without You," by LeAnn Rimes.

"It comes on the radio out of the blue," he says. "I know it's Nikki letting me know she's right there with me."

Nikki continues her mission of granting wishes for all of the children she meets. She is a force to be reckoned with, a force of love, strength, and courage. As I am writing her story, I can see her flying around with that wand in her hand, ready to make wishes come true. She is a beautiful soul who continues to spread love and light wherever she goes. May she be a shining example for us all.

Nikki's father shared some poems that Nikki wrote. I was so touched when I read them that I felt guided to share them with you. I hope they touch you as much as they did me.

Life
by Nikki Einhorn

Life is what
You live everyday
Some people are limited
Some people live forever

Some have days, years, decades
They are the lucky ones who
Are not limited

My Life
by Nikki Einhorn

I'm trapped in a time warp
Everyday repeating itself
I yell and I scream
I cry myself to sleep
Just thinking what
The next day would hold
Could kill me

Thank you, Nikki, for your wise words. May we resonate with them and know that life can sometimes seem unfair, but may your words serve as a reminder to be grateful for the time we have here on earth. May we envision you in that beautiful place called heaven where you continue to be the light for others both near and far. Shine bright, dear Nikki. I think I can see you from here.

Chapter 31

The Never-Ending Love Affair

I met an amazing woman named Marion who came to me seeking a connection with her late husband, Jim. He had passed just a short time before we met, and although she felt him close by on a regular basis, Marion wanted validation that what she was experiencing was, in fact, her husband coming to her in various and amazing ways. Marion was such a sweet and gentle soul. She was full of smiles when she arrived at my place, and I could feel the excitement welling up inside of her. I showed her to the room where her reading would take place, gave her a few instructions, and opened with a prayer.

Marion's husband came riding in to the reading on his Harley. He was a vibrant and joyous soul. "He's riding his Harley," I told her.

Marion just beamed as the words flowed from my mouth. Jim began to reminisce about their riding days. What fun they had!

"Those were some of the best days of his life," I told her. Marion agreed.

"Have you noticed a cardinal?" I asked her. "Jim is showing me a cardinal and says that he comes around often." Marion nodded her head and said that she saw them all of the time.

"I'm not surprised he chose a cardinal," Marion said. "They're such beautiful birds."

I told Marion that I saw Jim smoking. "He says that you smell it from time to time. It's him," I said.

She answered with a quick, "Yes, I do smell the smoke occasionally."

"Oh, he loves you so much," I continued. "You were true soul mates."

Marion nodded her head and said, "Yes, we definitely were."

I saw Marion being given an American flag as she went to pick up her husband's ashes. She acknowledged this as so and told me that Jim was a Korean War vet.

"They did give me a flag when I went to pick up his ashes," she continued.

As the reading progressed, I told Marion that her husband often whispered "sweet nothings" in her ear and that it might feel like a sort of tingling sensation. Marion looked surprised and said that this had been happening ever since he had passed.

"It's been driving me nuts," she said. "Now I know it's just Jim telling me how much he loves me. I'm okay with that." Marion giggled like a little girl as she realized that Jim was still telling her how much she meant to him.

Marion and Jim were together for sixty-one years and married for fifty-nine of them. Marion told me that they had such a wonderful marriage—not to say they didn't have any disagreements, but they loved each other so much that they made things work. I hear from Marion from time to time and she says that she continues to receive visits from Jim. She says he visits as the little cardinal and sits with her during her morning and evening prayers. She says that she often smells the smoke from his pipe as she prays.

"He finds ways to pick me up when I'm feeling low," she told me during one conversation. Marion recalled one occasion when she was feeling quite lonely. She decided to turn on the radio and tuned it to a fifties station. The first song that came on was "Pennies from Heaven," which brought a smile to Marion's face, as she just knew it was Jim's doing. After listening for a while, she got up to turn the radio off, but before she was able to turn the knob, another familiar song began to play. It was "Be My Love" by Mario Lanza, and it was "their song"—the one they had deemed as theirs when they had started dating so many years ago.

Marion reports that Jim has helped several family members avoid harm on different occasions. Once, when Marion was experiencing some difficulty with her balance, Jim came to her rescue. She placed a chair by her front door where she always took her shoes off. One day, she sat down to take her shoes off, and upon standing, she completely lost her balance. Instead of falling flat on her face, which is what should've happened, according to Marion, her body was somehow turned, and she ended up facedown on the sofa. The sofa was approximately four feet away from the chair she had been sitting in. Marion knows in her heart that it was Jim who had saved her.

"He saved me from hitting my head on my buffet, which was right in front of me," she told me.

Marion's daughter has also experienced miracles by way of her father. One of hers happened while she was driving along a busy freeway. As she was coming around a long bend in the road in the left lane of a three-lane highway, her car was suddenly moved very gently to the right-hand side. Marion said that her daughter could actually feel the car move, and she wasn't steering it in that direction. She glanced over to the left lane where she had been just a few moments before, only to see a car that had drifted into her lane at a very fast pace. She realized that if her car hadn't moved to the right, she would've been hit by that car!

Marion and her daughter talk with Jim regularly. They ask him for guidance and support, and they trust that he will answer their call. They are open to all of the miraculous ways that he is able to come to them and help them. Because of this, I believe they have opened the floodgates to unlimited possibilities. Jim has been, and will always be, able to let them know he is near in one way or another.

Chapter 32

Finding Love Again

As our loved ones spend their time in heaven, they constantly think of ways to help us as our journeys continue here on earth. They work diligently in our favor, opening doors to new possibilities and opportunities. This is especially true for those who have lost significant others, soul mates, true loves, whatever you may call your beloved. Clients are often surprised as their loved one comes forth with messages of "new love," coming forward with supportive nudges for their grieving partners to find love again. It pains them to watch us continue on alone with the idea that we would be dishonoring them by loving someone else. That's just one of the many reasons people may resist finding love again, but it's one of the most common that I have connected with.

One thing that I can assure you is that your beloved only wants you to be happy. And for those of you who have lost your lovers, spouses, and soul mates, that often means that you must love again. Not only to receive love, but to give it to someone else. It might blow you away to know that your beloved will even help you find the perfect person, the perfect one to take his or her place. But who else knows you better? They, along with your angels, will orchestrate chance meetings and coincidences, ensuring that you meet your new love at the perfect moment. Of course, although they have all of this set up for you, it is ultimately up to you whether or not you actually meet your new love. You must be open to the idea of loving again, and you must let them know that you are ready. They won't be angry with you—quite the contrary. All they wish for you is to be happy as you finish your time here on earth. They wait patiently for you to let them know that you are ready to love again, and they can make magic occur as soon as you do.

The following are a few examples of how loved ones helped some of my clients find love again. This is just a small sample of hundreds of similar stories that have come across my path. I hope you can feel the unconditional love and support that came pouring down from their loved ones in heaven, as I did.

~Sally~

As I began a reading for a woman named Sally, her husband came in without any hesitation. I'm often able to tune into a soul's energy, and Jack's was so loving and kind. I smiled at Sally and told her that her husband was an amazing man. "Gentle Giant is what I want to call him," I told her as I smiled. Sally nodded her head and said that that fit him to a T. Jack talked about their children and many grandchildren, offering detailed information about each of them. Sally beamed as she listened to her husband talk about all of the things she thought he had missed.

"I can't believe he's seen it all," she said with relief.

"Oh, he said to assure you that he hasn't missed a thing," I replied. I could feel the amazing love they shared, and it was evident that Jack was the love of her life.

As the reading continued, I told Sally that Jack loved her so much but that he didn't want her to be alone. "He says you're going to be here for a long time and that you're not supposed to spend it alone." He wanted her to know that she was the love of his life, but that there was someone else who could love her just as much as he did. He had the perfect person already picked out for Sally. All she needed to do was be open to loving someone again. Sally wept as she heard what her husband was saying. She missed him so much, but I could feel the pain in her heart as she continued life alone. I told Sally that our loved ones truly want us to be happy, and that they know whether or not we would be happy with someone else. I told her that I understood that it all might sound crazy, but that her husband would be okay with her loving someone else.

"He truly only wants you to be happy," I continued, "and he says that being alone isn't the answer." I told her how it would only cause Jack pain to see her continue her journey alone, as he could feel the emptiness in her heart.

After several minutes of tears, Sally admitted that she didn't want to be alone. She said that she had never looked for love again, as she felt it would be disrespectful of her husband. I told Sally that she and her husband shared something so special, something so many of us yearn for. I told her that although she had found her perfect soul mate and had been able to spend so many years with him, there were others whom she could find happiness with.

"It might not ever be the same as it was for you and Jack, but it can still be good," I relayed from her husband.

Sally's tears slowed down as she began to think of the possibility of opening her heart to love once more. She said she was excited about the thought of having someone in her life again, as she was so tired of going it alone. She giggled at the thought of her husband picking out the perfect person and said that that sounded just like him.

"I'm sure he would be very picky as to who was around his grandchildren," she said jokingly. I told her he was just as picky as to who would be taking care of his beautiful bride. Her eyes welled up once more as she gently shook her head yes. She was ready. She was ready to love again, and she knew that her beloved Jack would send her the perfect person.

Jack spoke of an upcoming cruise that Sally was going on. She validated this and said that it was planned for a couple of months later. I told her that I thought she would be meeting someone on the cruise and to just be open to the possibility. As the reading came to a close, I told Sally to remain open to all of the miracles that Jack could send her way. "He can do amazing things," I told her. "Just ask for what you want and get out of his way."

I heard from Sally about six months later. She had gone on that cruise and had indeed met someone new. They were dating and enjoying a wonderful and loving relationship. Sally said she knew that her husband, Jack, had something to do with it, as her new guy treated her just as special as he had.

~Sarah~

I met another woman, Sarah, who had lost her husband at a very young age. They had been married just ten years when he was taken in a head-on collision. They had been high school sweethearts and had married right after graduation. The love they shared was eternal, and I could feel the pain that she held in her heart. Her husband was such a sweet and gentle spirit. He came shining through with Archangel Michael standing by his side.

I began to see what had happened to him in those last moments. He was driving along, listening to the radio, anxious to get home to see his beautiful wife. He caught a glimpse of something coming toward him and was in disbelief as he realized what was about to happen. A car was speeding toward him, out of control. At that instant, the moment he saw the car coming at him, Archangel Michael reached into his car and pulled him out. Archangel Michael had plucked his soul from that car right before the impact. Her husband stood by Archangel Michael and watched the whole thing happen.

"Archangel Michael spared your husband all of the pain and trauma of what was going to happen," I told Sarah. "Your husband stood there and watched the whole thing." I began to describe the color of her husband's car, as well as that of the car that had hit him. She validated that my descriptions were accurate. I even described what the car looked like after it had been mangled so terribly.

"Your husband wants you to know that he didn't suffer. He says he was just as surprised as you are, hearing this today." I continued and told Sarah how our angels are able to spare us from pain and trauma and that her husband didn't suffer.

"That has always weighed on me," Sarah said. "I am so relieved that he didn't suffer. That helps more than you could ever know."

As the reading continued, Sarah's husband brought up her new love interest. Sarah seemed surprised and a little nervous when he began talking about her new man.

"Who's Chris?" I asked her, to which she replied, "my new love interest."

We both giggled and waited to see what Sarah's husband had to say about that. After a few moments, I said, "Your husband says that he was the one who set this all up between you and Chris. He says he's the perfect guy for you." Sarah's eyes filled up and tears began to flow down her face as she explained that Chris was her husband's best friend. He and Sarah had leaned on each other after her husband's passing and had grieved together. She went on to explain that after time, something started to happen. She and Chris began to develop feelings for one another. Sarah continued to weep as she said she felt so guilty for the feelings she now had for her husband's best friend.

"I never felt this way about Chris when my husband was alive, and I want him to know that," she kept repeating as she sobbed.

I placed my hand on Sarah's shoulder and said, "Honey, he knows that. Your husband brought the two of you together because he knew you were perfect for each other. He only wants you to be happy now," I continued. Sarah's husband only wanted the best for her, and he knew that Chris was the one. Sarah continued to cry, but her tears had now shifted from tears of sadness to tears of joy. She told me that she had a feeling that her husband had something to do with all of it.

"That's how much he loved me," she said.

Sarah left her reading free of the guilt and shame she had been carrying for so long. She knew that her husband had made sure that she was taken care of and that she was with someone who would love her as much as he did. She knew that he had made something magical happen between she and Chris, and she was grateful for her husband's love and support. Sarah waved as I watched her get into her car that afternoon. The smile on her face said it all. I knew she ready to start the next chapter, and I knew it was going to be amazing.

If you are like Sally or Sarah and are struggling with the thoughts of loving someone else after losing your loved one, please know that your loved one truly only wants you to be happy. Quite often, that means that they don't want you to be alone as they wait to greet you in heaven some day. Personally, I have never connected with anyone in heaven who wishes that his or her beloved remain alone. It's actually the opposite, as they know we continue to have the desire to give and receive love with another. Just know that you will not only have their blessing, but their help as well, if you decide to allow your heart to love again. Ask your departed loved one to bring you the perfect mate. I mean, really, who knows you better?

Chapter 33

Voices from the Other Side

I encourage clients to record their sessions so that they can listen to them from time to time, if needed. My readings are jam-packed with so much information that I don't want them to miss a thing. That was my intent in the beginning, but as I began to give more and more readings, things began to shift. Several people began contacting me after returning home and listening to their reading to report that there was something else or someone else on the recording. It wasn't just my voice or my client's voice that was audible. They often hear voices and sometimes even what they describe as "angelic sounds" coming over the recording that weren't audible during the actual reading. These voices are often deceased loved ones and guides, offering support and guidance at pivotal times during readings. Although I have done thousands of readings, I have only heard from a select few who have heard these unexplainable voices and sounds on their recording. I've even had the privilege of listening to some of them and am absolutely blown away each and every time. It never ceases to amaze me how our loved ones and guides can come to us in miraculous ways. The next few stories are individual accounts of some of my clients who experienced this amazing phenomenon.

~The Grandmother's Call~

I did a reading for a young woman who was around twenty years old. She had come to me hoping to connect with her beloved grandma, whom she missed so terribly. Kimberly arrived with a recorder in hand. She was eager to hear from her grandmother and wanted to make sure she didn't miss a thing.

"I want to record my session so that I can listen to it again later," she said.

I nodded my head in agreement and told her to begin recording. I opened the reading with a prayer, calling in all of Kimberly's loved ones, angels, and guides and asked that the messages she received be for the highest good of all.

As Kim's reading began, loved ones started to pour in. Although she had several loved ones who peeked in to say hello, her grandmother wasted no time in taking control of the reigns.

"Your grandmother loves you so much," I told Kimberly. "She says you were like sisters," I said as I giggled.

Kim nodded her head and acknowledged that they had had a relationship that was more like that of sisters than of a grandmother and granddaughter.

"Your grandma is showing me three of you. Three girls. You used to have such a good time together," I continued. Kimberly once again nodded her head yes and said that she had two sisters.

"We all used to hang out with my grandma all the time. We would fix each other's hair and just laugh all day long."

"Well, your grandma wants you to know that she is still hanging out with all of you. She's still one of the girls," I assured her.

This brought a smile to Kim's face, as she knew that her grandmother was reassuring her that she would always be close.

About halfway through Kim's reading, she asked about a lifelong friend.

"I have this friend that I'm worried about," Kim said. "I wonder if you could tell me anything about him."

I tuned in for a moment and then proceeded with what I was receiving.

"I see that your friend is making some bad choices," I told her. "He's dabbling in drugs, and things are starting to get out of control." Kim nodded her head yes and said that her friend was indeed dabbling in drugs.

"I'm just so worried about him. Is there anything I can do?" she asked.

This young man's grandmother, who had passed the previous year, began to come through. "His grandmother says that she is watching over him closely," I told her. "She says that they were super close and that she loves him so much. She's worried about where he is headed," I continued.

I told Kim that I saw this beautiful grandmother hugging her grandson, trying to get him to notice that she was near.

"She hugs him all the time," I said. "She's squeezing him so tight in the hopes that he'll be able to feel her."

Kimberly seemed relieved.

"I'm glad his grandmother is watching over him," she said. "I pray for him all the time."

Kim's reading continued, and I received a plethora of information for her. She received guidance about her future, including specific things about her love life, career, future children, and even information about a future move. Kim even received messages for her sisters and couldn't wait to share what she had gotten with them. As Kim's reading came to a close she gave me a great big hug and thanked me for her reading. She said she felt so much more peaceful and calm and was thrilled to know that her grandmother was still with her.

"I know everything's going to be okay now," she said as she walked out the door.

To my surprise, I received a message from Kim a few days later. She sent a brief text that said, "Listen to this," with an audioclip attached. I had no idea what to expect but was eager to take a listen to it. As I listened to the recording, I realized that it was a brief clip from her reading. In the clip, Kim and I had just finished talking about her friend, whom she was worried about, and had moved on to some information I was receiving about her sister's future children. As I paused in-between sentences, a voice called out over the recording saying, "Tom." It sounded like an older woman's voice, and it was clear as a bell. And the kicker was that Tom was the name of Kim's friend. He was the one that she had asked about, the one who had been dabbling in drugs. My client sent me another message and told me that she had called Tom over to listen to her reading. She said he became very emotional when he heard his name and claimed it was his grandmother's voice. Although I don't know what ever happened with Tom, I can't help to think that maybe, just maybe, he was able to walk away from drugs after hearing his sweet grandmother's voice calling from the other side. How truly amazing that this sweet little lady was able to call out to him.

~The Native's Chants~

I saw a woman who had been struggling for so long. Donna came into my studio broken and beaten down, in search of anything that might help her find some new direction. It was apparent that she was hitting rock bottom, as her weathered face told the whole story. I summoned Donna's loved ones, angels, and guides and asked them to come through with divine guidance for her.

"We are asking for miracles today," I said during the opening prayer. And with that, Donna's amazing reading began.

It became clear from the get-go that Donna was stuck in victimhood. She had lived a life of powerlessness and had a pattern of picking partners that ensured that she stay in that role and never even dream of changing. I told Donna over and over that the angels were standing behind her, helping her find her strength and her voice.

"You have so many," I told her. "They have always been there and promise you that they aren't going anywhere. Your guides say that it is time for you to be assertive. They know this might be difficult for you, but they want to assure you that they will help you." As I looked at my client who was sitting directly across my little table from me, I saw Archangel Michael standing right behind her.

"Archangel Michael is right behind you and is nudging you to take a stand," I said. "He's been trying to fill you up with strength and courage so that you can finally take a step toward happiness."

As Donna's reading came to a close, her demeanor changed a bit. It wasn't as dramatic as I'd seen for others, but I could see a glimmer of hope in her eyes that wasn't there before. I closed with a prayer and asked the angels to surround Donna with love, strength, and courage. I hugged her and told her that there were amazing things waiting for her and that all she needed to do was to take the first step.

I'm not sure if Donna was ever able to take that first step, that step to freedom and happiness, but I did hear from one of her family members a few weeks after her reading. When Donna went home and listened to her recording, she heard voices chanting in the background. She was shocked at what she was hearing and called some family members and asked them to come over and listen for themselves. They were stunned. During the reading, at the moment where I was telling Donna that it was time for her to be more assertive, they could hear what sounded like Native Americans chanting in the background. It sounded like there were several of them and they were chanting, "Be assertive, be assertive, be assertive." Crazy, right? I know! I can't help but think that it was Donna's tribe sending love and support, letting her know that she was not alone.

~Those Darn Waywards~

Some cool things happened during one particular small-group reading that I did. The group was held in a private home, and there were eight women from the same family who attended. As always, I suggested the family record the session in hopes that they might hear their loved ones and guides. The homeowner got up and placed a small recorder in the middle of the circle we had made. I began the reading with my usual prayer, calling in all of our beings of light, angels, guides, and any deceased loved ones that wanted to come forward with loving and supportive messages. The one family member that they all wished to connect with came in immediately. She had actually connected with me all day, as she was so eager to let them all know she was okay. When she was living, Mary had played the role of aunt, sister, and mother to these eight women, and to say she was missed was an understatement. Mary had played such a huge role in all of these women's lives and was the rock for the entire family. As soon as she came through, everyone began to cry.

"We miss her so much," one of the girls said while choking back tears. Mary would deliver many profound messages that afternoon—messages that put her loved ones at ease and let them know she was still with them every waking moment.

About halfway through the reading, I felt as if Mary was urging me to point out the recorder. As I pointed down at the small digital recorder lying in front of me, I said, "Mary says that you're going to hear something, other than me. She says to pay attention to it." I giggled a bit and looked upward, as if I was looking up at Mary, and said, "You'd better make that happen since you made such a big deal about it." We all laughed, and the reading continued.

As the reading progressed, I began to receive information that there were some uninvited guests hanging out in the home we were in. There were several what I refer to as "waywards" running about the house, wreaking havoc on everyone who lived there. I'm sure it's just some sort of symbol for me, but I see waywards as little gargoyle-looking things. They are made up of lower energies like fear, anger, resentment, grief, and sadness, and they enjoy forcing these feelings onto those they coexist with. When waywards are present, one may experience headaches, sleeplessness, overwhelming sadness, fear, or anger without any valid reason. Although you wouldn't know it from my description of them, waywards are very easy to get rid of. They are just ornery little things that enjoy wreaking havoc on the humans around them, as they seem to get such enjoyment out of watching us struggle.

I asked the homeowner if she ever heard things scurrying about, and she answered, "Yes. All the time."

I explained how these waywards had been affecting everyone in the home, making them emotional and drained. She acknowledged that with every word, I seemed to be describing her entire family.

"Once we clear them, everything will get better. Are you ready to clear these little pests?" I asked, to which she immediately replied, "Yes!"

I asked the group to close their eyes and I asked God to shine His light into the home and around the home. I asked Jesus and Archangel Michael to come in and find anything of lower energy that needed to go to the light. I asked Archangel Michael to bring his sacred vacuum into the home, particularly to the basement, and take any and all waywards up into the light. I often see Archangel Michael scolding waywards as he rounds them up, almost like he is scolding little kids who are getting into mischief. I've even heard him telling these waywards things like, "How dare you do this to this family," and, "You should be ashamed of yourself." Once Archangel Michael gets a hold of them, waywards always look like little kids who just got in really big trouble. They walk with their heads down, dragging their feet as they walk to the light. Believe me, it's quite a sight to see! Once I heard the familiar "all-clear" from Archangel Michael, I told the homeowner that her house was clear. She thanked me, and we continued with the group reading.

I received a message from the homeowner a couple of days later. She said that her family had listened to the recording and that they did hear someone else's voice besides mine on the recording. At the point where I begin to bring everyone's attention to the recording device, when Mary had me point at it, you can hear a soft voice in the background say, "It's real." Then, when I tell the homeowner that Archangel Michael has gathered up all of the waywards and that her house is clear, you can hear, "We're done here." Wow! You can't get any more specific than that. Again, just amazing proof of how our loved ones, angels, and guides can validate things for us.

~A Mother's Call to Her Daughter~

And here's just one more really quick, yet amazing story. I did a reading for a young woman who was able to connect with her mother, whom she had just lost within the previous year. During my client's reading, her mother came in with so many supportive and loving messages. She mentioned things from the past and present as well as offering hope for the future. Amber left her reading thrilled to have been able to connect with her mom. She thanked me for everything and headed toward her car.

I heard from Amber a few days later when she left a message on my voicemail. Her message said, "I can't thank you enough for my reading the other day. When you called on the angels and asked them to open the gates so that my mother could say something to me, I heard my name. My mother said my name."

Just as with all of the other times before, Amber's message blew me away. Although I've had the privilege of listening to several clients' recorded readings and have heard voices from the other side, it never ceases to amaze me. Our loved ones, angels, and guides can do so much if we simply ask and believe.

Chapter 34

Alzheimer's and Dementia

I've done many readings for people where the subject of Alzheimer's or dementia were brought up by their loved ones in heaven. So many struggle as they watch their loved one, often a parent, drift off into a place of oblivion. Those left behind who are faced with making heartrending decisions are often riddled with guilt and shame. The burden they carry extends to thoughts that they are not only letting down their loved one who is afflicted with such diagnoses, but that they also might be judged by those who are in heaven looking down. The following stories are just a snippet of the many readings I've done for people who are experiencing similar circumstances. I hope that after you read them, you are able to realize that there is so much more going on behind the scenes—so much more than we ever could have imagined!

~The Train Rides~

I met with an amazing Earth Angel named Rosa. She was petite and round, with a smile that reached from ear to ear. As Rosa entered my home, I could feel the love that filled her heart. She was such a beautiful person, inside and out. As I began her reading, I immediately heard that she was an Earth Angel, and I told her what I was receiving. I told her that she had dedicated her life to helping others, in any way, shape, or form. She agreed. Rosa's father, who had passed ten years before, began to come with loving messages.

"Does your mother have Alzheimer's?" I asked, to which Rosa replied yes. I asked if she was in a nursing home or something similar, and she replied yes once again. Rosa began to cry, and I could feel the anguish in her heart.

"You feel guilty for her being there," I said. Rosa nodded her head as she held her face in her hands and sobbed. As I continued to receive guidance, I told Rosa that her father loved her so much.

"He is so proud of you, and he wants you to know that you did all you could. There was no other choice," I continued. Rosa's father began to show me how he took Rosa's mother on journeys while she slept. "He takes her to see beautiful places when she's sleeping soundly," I told her. I asked Rosa, and she acknowledged that she did indeed find her mother sleeping so soundly at times that she would check to see if she was still breathing.

"It happens a lot," she said. She went on to say that she had even mentioned it to her mother's nurse that very morning. "She was sleeping so soundly that I actually thought she wasn't breathing. I spoke with the nurse, and she assured me that my mother was just sleeping."

Rosa's father began to show me that he often came and took her mother on journeys. He showed me that they would go on train rides all over the country, visiting different destinations and taking in the sights. Rosa's eyes began to tear up as she explained that her parents loved to ride the train and had done it for many years, until her father's passing. I asked Rosa if she ever noticed her mother mumbling under her breath, sometimes while awake but also while sleeping. She said that yes, she did it often.

"She's talking to your father," I said, "while they are on these adventures." Rosa's face started to change as she began to realize that, just possibly, her mother wasn't stuck in that body and mind that no longer worked so well. As the movie continued in my head, I told Rosa that her father also took her mother up to heaven to see what was waiting for her. Other loved ones came through, and I began rattling off names that Rosa recognized. There were uncles and aunts, grandparents, friends, and so many others. I watched as Rosa's mother would travel to heaven and meet them again while on these journeys. There was so much joy and laughter as her family sat around a large, round table reminiscing of days gone by. I was able to give Rosa specific things that had happened within the family since her father's passing. Rosa was astonished and just kept giggling as I continued with everything I was seeing. She was so delighted to know that her father had seen everything. As Rosa's reading came to a close, I told her that her mother was being taken care of.

"Your father wants you to know that he is watching over her. He continues to take her on train rides to magical places and will continue to take her on amazing journeys as long as she is still here on earth." I reassured Rosa that she had no reason to feel guilty, and that her mother was having the time of her life while she slept.

"She's just not able to tell you all about it," I told Rosa. "She is seeing amazing things."

Rosa felt so relieved to know that her mother wasn't suffering, as she had thought she was. She was so happy to know that her father was right by her mother's side. She wasn't alone, and better yet, she wasn't stuck in that body that lay in the nursing home.

"I feel so much better," Rosa said as we hugged good-bye. "I should've known my father would never let my mom just lay there. That just wasn't their style."

~Here Comes Johnnie~

I met with three sisters for a small group reading. They were seeking a connection with loved ones who had passed, as well as any guidance their angels and guides might have for them. I opened with a prayer, calling in God and the angels, as well as any guides and deceased loved ones who came with messages of love, healing, and guidance. "Johnnie's here" came through front and center. I told the women that there was a jolly man coming forward, smoking a cigar. He was quite a character, and I knew that this was their father. The women all grabbed tissues as the tears began to flow. I told them that their father kept saying, "Here comes Johnnie," and they all began laughing.

"He said that all the time," one of his daughters replied.

"Who's Simona," I asked.

The women got quiet and one of them answered, "She's our mother." I began to see their mother the same way I see others who have Alzheimer's and dementia. I asked if she had either of those conditions, and they replied yes.

"Your father loves your mother so much," I told them. I began to see their mother and father dancing and said, "He takes her dancing while she sleeps. They're having so much fun."

All three women burst into tears. They all cried uncontrollably for a few moments. When they were finally able to calm down, one of the women began to tell me how their parents were such amazing dancers.

"They won all kinds of competitions all over the state."

I told the women that their father wanted to reassure them that he was watching over their mother. I asked them if she had actually called out his name recently, as that was what their father was showing me.

One of the sisters exclaimed, "Yes, it just happened the other day."

"Your father wants to assure you that she did see him," I said. The three sisters appeared to have some sort of calmness come over them as I continued talking about all of the magical things their father was capable of.

"He comes as a cardinal," I told them. The sisters all looked at each other in disbelief as they told me that a cardinal had appeared recently ... to all of them.

"That damn cardinal is everywhere," one of them said.

"It's your father," I told them. "He's trying to let you know that everything is going to be okay."

The three of them hugged and laughed as tears continued to flow down their faces.

"I knew Daddy wouldn't ever leave Mommy," one of them said to the others.

What a sense of relief for these sisters to know that their father was watching over their mother, Simona. Not only did it bring them some relief knowing that their mother and father were still dancing, but it also allowed them to let go of any guilt of not being able to be with their mother at all times. She was in good hands. Johnnie was making sure of that.

Chapter 35

What Happens in Hospice

I've done several readings over the years involving loved ones who are in hospice. As loved ones watch their family member drift off into an unknown place of stillness and unresponsiveness, they are left wondering what their loved one is experiencing, if anything, and if he or she is suffering or afraid. I hope the next story might somehow put some of your minds at ease.

I received a call from a family as they were preparing for their loved one to return home to heaven. Ed had been in hospice for about seven days when I received the call. His family had watched him as he faded into stillness and wondered who, if anyone, was there to help him get home. One of Ed's daughters called me and said that she had heard about me. She wondered if I would be available to do a reading over the phone that evening, as she, her sister, and her mother were desperate to know that Ed was okay.

"He's been in hospice for seven days now and he's unresponsive. We just want to know that he is okay," she said.

I just happened to be free that evening and agreed to speak with them. I told her that I would call around seven-thirty and we would see what we could find out. This was the first time I had ever been asked to connect with someone who was in transition, and I will have to admit that I was a bit nervous, not knowing what to expect. I was reassured with knowing that I had the ability to connect with an individual's higher self, something I had done on several occasions, but this was different. I was going to be connecting with someone who was on the cusp of leaving the physical plane, and this was new territory for me. Although I was nervous inside, I have to admit that I was eager to see what would happen.

I called the family later that evening and we started their reading. I opened with a prayer calling in God, the angels, and any beings of light with loving messages for the family. I took a deep breath and dove right in. As the reading began, I connected with Ed instantly. He came in quickly and easily and began to show me so many family members that he was with. He talked of his father and said that his dad was "showing him the ropes," something the family acknowledged was a familiar saying of his. I told Ed's wife that I could hear the angels singing Ed home.

"They sound so beautiful," I told her. "They are so happy to see him again. And you had something to do with it. The angels said that you asked them to come for him. They heard your call."

Ed's wife answered back over the line, "Thank you, angels. I knew you would come for him."

I continued and told them that Ed's soul had already left his body, but that his body just hadn't shut down yet. I described Ed lying in the bed, as he showed me what it looked like. As always, the movie was rolling in my head, and I was able to see everything. I told the family that his breathing was labored and I saw that he'd had cancer that had spread to his brain. The women on the other line validated this to be true.

"Ed keeps saying that he's sorry. He didn't mean the things he said. It was the cancer, not him," I told his wife as I began to hear words come from his mouth that just weren't like him. She replied that she knew it wasn't him, as he would never have said the things he did.

"Archangel Michael came for Ed. He's with spirit now," I told the three of them as I saw a white dove come into the picture, my sign that a soul is with spirit.

"Ed keeps whispering in your ear," I told his wife. "I can't make it out, but he says that your heart will know what he's saying."

Ed's wife said that although his body was still going, she had felt that his soul had left a couple of days before.

"This all makes sense," she said. "I have felt him around me a lot today."

I continued with what I was receiving and said, "Ed wants to thank you for giving him such a wonderful life and beautiful home. He wants you to know that he's with the child that the two of you lost many years ago." Ed's wife seemed relieved upon hearing this and proceeded to tell me that she had had a miscarriage several years before.

"I'm so happy he's with our baby," she said.

Throughout the reading, Ed often addressed his stepdaughters as "my girls," something they said he called them often. Although Ed had been a stepfather to his wife's two girls, he'd always treated them as if they were his own.

"He loves you girls so much," I told the two girls. "You were the best daughters anyone could ever have." The girls on the other end began sniffling, and I could tell that the words they were hearing meant a great deal.

"Ed mentioned his grandson and said that he would continue to guide him. No worries," I told them. "Ed's not going to let anything happen to him."

As I was relaying what I was hearing, Ed began to correct me. "He keeps telling me to call him Buddy, not Ed," I said.

"Oh, my gosh!" his wife exclaimed. "That was his nickname." We all giggled for a bit as we waiting for anything more from Ed.

"Ed says that the three of you have to lean on each other now. He knows that he was your rock, and he will be giving you all support from the other side," I told them. "He wants you to know that whatever his body appears to be going through, he is already in the light and is not suffering anymore."

Ed's wife and daughters were relieved to hear this, as they, of course, found it difficult to watch him lying in that bed so helpless.

"He says that whatever sounds you hear are just his body shutting down. He wants to assure you that he's not in any pain or discomfort anymore," I continued. Ed wasn't finished yet, and I continued to relay several more messages.

"Ed wants to apologize for ignoring the signs," I told them. "I mean, he is so sorry," I added. It turned out that Ed had been sick for a while but hadn't done anything about it.

"Yes, I know he is," his wife said gently.

"He's showing me a big, black dog sitting next to him," I continued.

"Oh, my gosh, that's Caesar!" one of his daughters exclaimed.

"Ed says that he just started laughing when he saw that big dog running toward him when he got there. He was so happy to see his old pal."

My connection with Ed was so amazing and seemed to go on and on. He spoke of others that were with him in heaven, including friends and family, and he even gave their names. He told his wife and daughters to be open to all of the miraculous ways that he would be able to let them know that he was still around them. He said they would see sparkles of light, a cardinal, and even rainbows from time to time. He told his wife and daughters that he would be lining everything up for them and that they were to be sure to let him know what they wanted.

"And he says to dream big," I told them.

He called his wife his "sweet angel" and thanked her for calling the angels in to take him home. "He will love you forever," I told her.

And with that, their amazing reading came to an end. Ed had come through with exactly what his girls needed to hear. He was already in that glorious place we call heaven, but more importantly, he wasn't suffering anymore. I said a prayer thanking all of our beings of light that had helped with the reading. We all said our good-byes, and I asked the family to keep in touch.

"I can't wait to hear about all of the miraculous ways Ed lets you know he's around," I said as we ended our call.

I heard from Ed's family a few weeks later. They said they had received all of the signs that I had mentioned during our reading. One of his daughters saw little sparkles of light just a short time after his passing and continues to see them from time to time. His wife and both girls saw the cardinal shortly after his passing and continue to see it on a regular basis.

"It often shows up when we need it most," one of the girls told me during a conversation. "We know it's Ed letting us know that everything is going to be okay."

They report that they have even seen the rainbow on many occasions. His grandson, Joey, who he promised to watch over, often comments that he sees rainbows in water puddles on the ground. Ed's wife feels him near all of the time and reports that their dog, Cooper, who is still living, often drops his toy by Ed's chair.

"I can feel Ed sitting in his chair," she told me, "and I know Cooper senses his presence."

Ed passed on the second day of Saint Ann's Novena in 2012, a place that has served as a beacon of hope for many people. Saint Ann's Novena is the same place where Ed proposed to his wife in 1999.

Chapter 36

"Crazy Legs" George

I met a woman named Barbara who had lost her husband just three weeks before we spoke. She lost her husband, George, after a long and difficult battle with Parkinson's. They met late in life and had been married for only a couple of months when he began exhibiting symptoms. Although I'm sure they both felt cheated in some way, they made the best of their situation and shared a love that many of us dream of.

When I spoke with Barbara, she was so broken and lost and could barely keep from crying. She said that she had had a beautiful dream about George three days after his passing. In the dream, he was standing right in front of her and was walking back and forth, as if he was showing her that he was able to walk again. George had lost the use of his legs, and Barbara was thrilled to see that they were working once again. In the dream, George made a reference to a punch line of one of his favorite jokes: "Don't believe everything you read." His family had been talking about this very joke on the day of his passing, and Barbara knew that by George bringing up the joke, he had heard everything they had said.

Since George's passing, Barbara had also experienced the feeling of him lying with her in bed, holding her.

"I can't exactly explain what happens. It's some sort of energy or something, but I know it's George, and he's actually holding me," Barb described. This is something that George has continued to do, and

Barbara reports that the energy has changed over time. What started out as feeling like some sort of energy around her shifted to a sort of tingling sensation to almost the point where she feels as if she has heavy towels on her arms. She chalks that heavy feeling up to George wrapping his arms around her.

During Barbara's initial reading, one of the things the George came through with was a baseball.

"He keeps showing me a baseball," I told her. Barbara proceeded to tell me that she and George were avid baseball fans. One day, when they were attending baseball game, George turned to Barbara and handed her a baseball. On it, George had written, "Barbara, will you marry me?" Barbara giggled as the memory of that day came flooding back in. George continued bringing in so many loving and supportive messages for Barb.

"He just keeps dancing around so silly. He's so happy that his legs work again," I said. Barbara was thrilled to know that George had the use of his legs again.

"That was so difficult for him," she said.

After our initial reading, Barbara began to receive more visits from George. One day, as Barb was cleaning out a closet, she noticed a baseball that George's coworkers had signed for him. She grabbed the ball and threw it to one of her dogs and told her pup to have fun with it. A couple of days later, as Barbara was getting ready to go to bed, she heard a small thud followed by what sounded like something rolling across the floor. She went downstairs to see what it was, only to find that very baseball sitting in the middle of the living room floor. It couldn't have been any of her dogs, as they were all upstairs in her bedroom already. She knew immediately that it was George just letting her know that he was there watching over all of them.

Barbara often hears songs on the radio that were special to the two of them.

"George always seems to send just the perfect song for me when I'm having a bad day," she told me. The fifties were George's favorite time for music, and he and Barb shared a love of cars.

175

"I occasionally see a car from the fifties roll past me, and I always feel it is George letting me know he's with me at that very moment." George kisses Barb often, and she reports that she can actually feel the prick of his beard. He comes as a cardinal periodically and will stay perched on a tree in her yard for long periods of time.

"I love that little bird," Barbara says. "I talk to him as if it's George standing right there."

During one of Barb's readings, her husband told her to purchase a book, *Animal Spirit Guides* by Steven Farmer. She said she couldn't wait to get it and planned to get it that very night. I told Barb that I saw butterflies and dragonflies and asked if they meant anything to her. She said that they didn't mean anything in particular, so I told her to just be open that something was going to happen involving butterflies and dragonflies. I received a telephone message from Barb the next day. She said that she had decided to take a walk at a nearby state park, something else her husband had suggested during her reading. As she walked, she began to notice several butterflies and dragonflies, and as she continued walking, she became completely surrounded by them.

"There were so many. I couldn't believe it," Barb told me. "And one dragonfly sat still on a rock right in front of me. It sat so still and just looked right at me."

Barb knew right away that it was just another sign from George, letting her know that he could do just about anything.

Barbara's connection with George seemed to progress over time. She reports a stronger connection not only with George but also with God, the angels, and the higher beings that she feels are guiding her. As time has progressed, her experiences have become more profound and intense. She even reports being able to hear one of her beloved dogs that passed away.

"Although it happens so quickly, I can hear her bark as clear as a bell. I don't know where it's coming from, but I know it's her," Barbara says.

After our initial reading, Barbara began meditating. She attributes her deeper connection to George, her dog, and all of her angels and guides to her daily meditation routine.

"I can't thank you enough for suggesting that I begin meditating," she told me. "It has changed my life in so many ways."

Since George's passing, Barbara has prayed to be by his side. She said she has always had a feeling that she wouldn't be here for a long time, which has only increased since George's passing. Barbara reports that she feels strongly that she will be with George very soon, but she has promised friends and family that she will leave it up to God as to when that is. Barb has always felt that she will have a peaceful passing and that George will be the one to come for her. She prays for that day to come, but until it does, she will continue to connect with George in whatever way she can.

"I'm just going to remain open to whatever magical ways George can let me know he's around," Barb told me. "I know he can do so much more than I could ever imagine. I'm ready to see what he can do."

Barbara isn't the only person I've spoken with who has a magical connection with a loved one who has passed. I've spoken with many widows and widowers who share similar experiences, each unique to their own circumstances. The connection that we can continue to share with our beloved can be truly amazing if we can remain open to unlimited possibilities and let go of control. Be open to the many ways your loved one can let you know he or she is near, and watch the miracles come flooding in.

Chapter 37

Michael's Miracle

I met a man who was seeking a connection with his wife, whom he had lost within the last year. Although Michael and Shannon had met later in life, they had developed a love that was stronger than what many share after many years of marriage. They had only been married a short time before Shannon was diagnosed with inoperable cancer. Her prognosis was grim and the cancer progressed rapidly. They were forced to say good-bye just two short years later.

During Michael's reading, Shannon came through with so much I could hardly keep up. It was obvious that she loved him, and the love they shared was truly amazing.

About halfway through Michael's reading, I looked up at him and said, "Your wife says that she saved you."

Michael's eyes filled with tears as he replied, "I know she did." Michael went on to tell me about a terrible accident he had been in several months before. He described his mangled car, stating that he should not have lived through the horrendous accident.

"I was broadsided by a huge truck with no warning. I shouldn't have made it," he told me. His vehicle was crumpled and smashed beyond what anyone could ever imagine, but Michael said that he walked away from the accident with barely a scratch. When he returned the next day to assess the damage, Michael noticed two long strands of blond hair on either side of the headrest where he had been sitting at the time the accident occurred. He knew instantly that it had been Shannon who had kept him safe, as that was the color of his wife's hair.

"I bought that car after she passed away," Michael told me. "Those two strands of hair were lying perfectly straight on either side of the headrest. I know she put them there so I would see them and know that she was the one who had saved me," he continued.

Michael said there have been a number of times that his beautiful Shannon has come to his aid. "I know she is acting as one of my guardian angels now," Michael reports, "and my love grows deeper for her with each and every day."

I spoke with Michael just before sending my book to my publisher. He said that he had found love again and that he had recently gotten married. I wasn't surprised, as Shannon had come in during his reading to tell him that she had the perfect person lined up for him.

"I'm so happy you found love again," I told him. "Shannon is smiling from ear to ear."

Chapter 38

The White Wolf

Over the years, I've done several readings where a majestic white wolf appears and offers guidance. This wolf comes in as a guide and protector and accompanies so many of us on our journey. Here are just a few stories about this amazing and loving guide.

I did a reading several years ago for a young woman who was expecting her first child. Katie was such a sweet girl who also had the gift of seeing and sensing spirit around her. She came seeking guidance about her life and welcomed anything that her angels and guides had to tell her. As Katie's reading began, I saw so many angels around her.

"You are so loved," I told her. "You have so many angels around you. I'm not sure I've ever seen this many before," I continued. As I began to receive more information, like that movie I see in my head, I began to see a little boy.

"You are going to have a little boy," I told Katie. "And he's going to be very sensitive."

I went on and told Katie how her son would be able to see spirits and angels and that he would be able to communicate with them. "He will be very sensitive to chemicals as well, and he's going to be a picky eater," I told her.

As the reading continued, I told Katie that her son was completely protected, just as she was. I saw that Archangel Michael would be keeping watch over him always, as he had an important job to do. He was going to be instrumental in spreading love and light, and he was coming to help make significant changes for the world around him. I began to see a white wolf lying by her son's crib.

"There's a white wolf that has been assigned to your son," I said. "He is going to be protecting him as well. The angels are showing me that you might hear growling on your son's monitor, but they want to assure you that it will only be the white wolf warning off any lower energies that might try to come near your son," I continued. "He will be a light for many. And that includes any spirits who haven't crossed over yet. They will be drawn to your son, as they know he can help them."

Some people might've just gotten up and ran right out the door upon hearing all of this, but Katie appeared relieved. She was quite intuitive and had a strong feeling that she was going to give birth to a very special little boy.

"I always felt that my son would be special. I just had no idea that he would be *that* special," she chuckled.

I heard from Katie several months later. She sent me an e-mail and told me that she had given birth to her beautiful little boy and that everything I had told her had come true. She stated that she even hears growling coming from his monitor from time to time, but she never feels frightened because she knows it is the white wolf watching over him. Katie said that she thanks Archangel Michael and the white wolf every single night for watching over her son. She knows that he is here to do great things and is ready to support him in any way that she can.

***

I did another reading for a woman named Amy. She was pregnant when we spoke and was about to give birth to a special child just like the one in the last story.

As Amy's reading began, I told her that she was going to give birth to a little girl and that she was going to name her Isabella.

Amy's eyes grew quite large as she said, "How did you know that"? It turns out that Amy was indeed having a girl and that she had already decided on the name Isabella.

"Your daughter is going to have the gift of sensing and seeing spirits and angels," I told her. Amy wasn't surprised at what she was hearing, as she and her son both had the ability to connect.

"Your daughter is even more gifted than your son," I told her. "Her connection is going to be even clearer than his."

Amy smiled as she listened to what the angels were saying. Her daughter was due in a few months, and she couldn't wait to hold her in her arms. About midway through Amy's reading, that white wolf began to appear. "There is a white wolf that will be coming as one of Isabella's guides and protectors," I said. "You might hear growling on your daughter's monitor from time to time, but the wolf wants you to know that it is only him. He will be keeping any lower energies away from your precious baby girl."

Amy seemed amazed at what she was hearing, but she was open to it all. "I'm so glad she has the wolf coming to protect her," Amy said. "I'll take all the help I can get!"

Amy contacted me several months later. Isabella was doing wonderful, and she was such a happy baby. Amy told me she had heard the growling. "It was crazy. I was up taking a shower and Bella was in her bouncy swing in another room. I heard something growling over the monitor and rushed in to check on her, but all she was doing was bouncing and giggling. It was as if she was playing with someone or something." Amy went on to say that she hears the growling from time to time, and when she checks on Bella, she is just as happy as can be. Amy knows that the white wolf is doing what he promised to do. He is keeping watch over her precious daughter as she finds her way in this world.

The white wolf comes through generally when I am conducting readings for someone who is expecting a child or for someone who has a young child already here. I decided to post something about it on one of the social media sites one day, in hopes of helping any parents who might be dealing with the same situation. I posted a beautiful picture of a white wolf lying under a blue moon and said something like, "This white wolf acts as a protector of many special children; you may hear him growling on occasion as he works to protect your child from any lower energies." The response was huge. I couldn't believe how many people responded to my post, saying either that they had heard the growling or that their child had mentioned seeing a white wolf. I even received responses from adults, thanking me for the post. The white wolf had acted as a protector to many of them when they were young. Some of them had even told me their stories of how they had told their parents of the white wolf, but they weren't believed.

"My parents never believed me," one gentleman wrote. "Thank you so much for posting this. This is the validation I needed."

I am so grateful that I was guided to post that message that day, as it reached so many people and helped them with their healing. We all have so many guides watching over us. For so many, it is the white wolf who guides and protects. At last, someone else knew about the white wolf, but more importantly, someone believed in it.

Chapter 39

Our Jobs in Heaven

When we leave this place here on earth and transition to our home once again, many of us continue with our work. I've done countless readings and connected with people who continued to do the things they loved so much here on earth. I've connected with grandmothers, teachers, musicians, and many others with gifts to share. Many of us continue doing what we did here on earth. We continue to mentor others; make everyone laugh; share our gift of song; spread cheer wherever we go. It's a beautiful place of peace and harmony, each soul helping the other to remain in a space of love. But I have to clarify something here. We don't all have jobs in heaven. I've connected with a number of souls who simply sit with family and friends who spend their time reminiscing about their time here on earth, recalling special moments and favorite events. There are no rules. It's a place of love. That is all.

The following are just a few examples of how many souls continue doing their "work" in heaven. I hope you enjoy hearing about them as much as I did when I connected with each of these beautiful beings.

~The Choir Director~

I met with a woman who came to me seeking connection and guidance. Carmen was in her early forties and was feeling absolutely lost and empty. She had seen me speak at an event and said that she knew she was supposed to come and see me.

"Something just kept telling me that you had answers for me," she said as we sat down for her reading. As usual, I began with a prayer calling in all of our angels, guides, and helpers and asked that she receive whatever she needed most for healing and moving forward.

"Your angels, guides, and loved ones know what that is," I assured her.

Carmen had several deceased loved ones come in during her reading. Her deceased husband, whom she had lost many years before, came through, as well as her mother, father, and several more family members. I was quite surprised at the number of people she had lost. She had been through much more than her fair share, and I could feel the pain that dwelled in her heart.

"I can't believe how many people you have in heaven," I remember saying to her. "I can't imagine what you've been through." Carmen began to sob as she heard my words.

"I have felt so alone for so long," she cried. Carmen was married now, but the love she once had for her new husband had begun to shift. "I just don't love him like I used to," she said. "But I feel so guilty for the way I feel because I know he still loves me so much."

"Your angels want you to know that it's okay that you have drifted apart. They want you to release any guilt or shame," I said. About that time, one of Carmen's family members stepped forward. Jim was a cousin who had recently passed from an aneurism in the brain. He was such a gentle and loving soul and was excited to connect with Carmen.

As Jim entered the reading, I felt so full of love and peace. I described a beautiful soul, someone who not only loved everyone but was loved by everyone. I described the way he looked, his mannerisms, and even said some of the phrases he was known to say. He came through with loving messages for Carmen and his own family as well.

"It's not your job to call them and tell them any of this," I told her. "It's just that you being here gives him the opportunity to come through with messages for anyone."

Jim came through and assured Carmen that he was at peace and in such a loving place. I began to see him in heaven, walking among the others.

"He's always smiling," I told her, which she said sounded just like him. I began to hear beautiful music and saw that Jim directed a choir.

"He's directing a choir of angels," I told her, "and they're all children." Carmen burst into tears. When she was able, she told me that her cousin Jim had been the choir director at her church.

"He just loved the children," she said while choking back tears.

"Well, he is continuing his amazing work in heaven," I said. "He so loves what he does, and he will continue to make a joyful noise." The two of us sat there for a moment, just looking at each other and smiling. We knew Jim was continuing his beautiful service in heaven. I began to hear a song inside my head. "I hear the song 'Amazing Grace,'" I told Carmen. "He says that's his favorite song."

Carmen's eyes filled up with tears once again, but she assured me they were tears of joy. "That was the song that was played at his funeral last month."

Carmen's reading didn't end there. Her husband came through with so much guidance and support. He commended her on doing such an amazing job raising their two children after his passing.

"He knows it hasn't been easy," I told her. "And he is so grateful for everything you have done."

Carmen's husband told her that it was time to be happy.

"Your husband says that it's time to think of you. He wants to help you be happy again." Carmen began to cry, and she told me that she just felt so stuck.

"I'm scared to make a change," she said. "I'm scared I'll make the wrong decision." As I waited for guidance from Carmen's husband and any of her angels, a clear picture began to come in my head.

"Are you thinking of moving away," I asked her, "to like Florida or something?"

Carmen looked at me with a surprised look on her face and replied, "Yes, I've been thinking about it." I continued with what I was receiving.

"Your husband said that your new love is waiting there for you. That's where you'll find the man of your dreams," I told her. "He's got everything lined up for you. All you need to do is take this step."

Carmen's demeanor seemed to change a bit, and I could see a glimmer of hope begin to shine from her beautiful brown eyes.

"Your husband says that the only wrong decision you can make is to not make one at all."

Carmen giggled and said, "That sounds just like him."

As Carmen's reading came to an end, she thanked me for helping her. "You have no idea what this reading has done for me," she said as she hugged me tight. "I can't thank you enough."

Carmen did end up leaving her husband and moving to Florida. It wasn't easy, but she knew it was something she just had to do. It was time for her, and it was time for her to be happy. Her divorce went smoothly, and although it was difficult for her to let go of any guilt and shame, she says she was able to do so with the angels' help.

"I called on them every single day and asked them to make things easy on me and my husband," she told me. "They answered my prayers."

I heard from Carmen again several months later. She had met the man of her dreams. Everything her husband had told her during her reading had come true, and she was living the life she had always dreamed of. She was finally happy, and she was so grateful she had taken a leap of faith. She knew that her husband and her many angels had helped her with everything and she knew that they would never leave her side. She felt so loved and knew that everything was going to be okay.

~The Grandmothers~

Over the years, I have done so many readings where I have connected with such amazing and loving grandmothers. They always come through with messages of love and support and are often kissing the cheeks of those sitting across from me at the table. There are so many grandmothers offering love and support in heaven. Not only do they continue to send you love and support here on earth, they also help those who are in need in heaven. Although there have been a plethora of readings where I connect with these beautiful souls, one in particular comes to mind right now.

I met with a young lady who desperately wanted to connect with her grandmother. This amazing woman had passed away just a few years back, and the loss my client felt in her heart was still as strong as it was when it happened. Jenny was so close to her grandmother, and what they had shared was more like a mother and daughter relationship. We began Jenny's reading with a prayer, calling upon God, Jesus, and any angels and deceased loved ones who had messages of love, clarity, and guidance for Jenny. Not surprisingly, Jenny's grandmother was the first to show up.

Her name was Rose, and she came in with such loving energy. I told Jenny that her grandmother had her arms around her and was hugging her so tight.

"She's hugging you so tightly, hoping you can feel it," I said. Jenny's cheeks had begun to turn red and she said she felt some sort of warm feeling going through her body.

"That's all of the love your grandmother is filling you up with," I replied. I felt so much love coming from her beloved grandma that I thought I was going to burst. Jenny's grandmother said that she had always felt like Jenny was her own daughter.

"She says that you were like a daughter to her and that the two of you were so close," I continued. Jenny nodded her eyes as tears began to well up in her eyes.

"I love her so much," Jenny said while wiping tears from her eyes.

"Your grandmother is showing me a bracelet. Does that mean anything to you?" I asked. She acknowledged that she did indeed have a bracelet and that her grandmother had given it to her right before her passing.

"I'm wearing it right now," she added as she pulled up her sleeve that had been covering it. Jenny began to smile as she felt the connection with her grandmother getting stronger.

"I can feel her here," Jenny said, "and I'm tingling all over."

"That's your grandmother here with us right now," I replied. "She's a strong energy, and she is so loving."

As Jenny's reading continued, her grandmother came through with so many messages for her beautiful granddaughter. I watched Jenny's whole demeanor change as I relayed message after message for her. She was beginning the shift from sadness and grief to a place of love and peace, something I'd watched happen so many times before. It truly never ceased to amaze me as I watched client after client make this shift, and I was grateful to be a part of Jenny's transition as well.

"I see your grandmother in heaven. There are so many children surrounding her," I told Jenny. "She finds the ones who haven't found their families yet and keeps them close to her until they do." Jenny listened while nodding her head from time to time as if acknowledging that everything I was telling her fit her grandmother to a T.

"She loves the children so much and takes such good care of them. It fills her with such joy to be around them," I added. Jenny smiled from ear to ear and said that her grandmother had always been known for "taking in the strays" when she was living.

"She welcomed anyone into her home and especially any kids who needed somewhere to go," Jenny said. "I'm so happy to know that she isn't alone and that she is able to continue doing what she so loved to do here when she was living."

Jenny was relieved to hear that her grandmother hadn't changed one bit. She continued to help others, just as she always had.

"Your grandma wants you to know that she's helping you too," I said. "She will never leave you." Jenny smiled in gratitude, and we closed her reading with a prayer of gratitude.

-The Guitar Player-

During a group reading one time, I remember connecting with a young man named David. He had passed a year before, and his sister was attending the reading in hopes that he would come through and connect with her. David was a beautiful spirit with such enthusiasm and joy in his heart.

"Your brother seems so fearless and wants you to know that he has no regrets. He lived his life to the fullest," I told her. As the reading continued, I was able to see that David had passed suddenly in a car accident. I told his sister that he had been spared any fear or pain, as Archangel Michael and his guardian angels had lifted his soul out of the car just before impact. I could see David standing there with his angels, watching the accident occur. I described the car and the tree that had claimed his life and told her how sorry I was for her loss. David's sister sat, crying, but she said that she felt so much better knowing that he hadn't suffered.

"That means a lot," she told me. "I just needed to know that he was okay."

As the vision shifted, I began to see David sitting on a beautiful, green lawn. He was in heaven.

"Your brother is sitting on a beautiful lawn and he's playing a guitar," I said. "There are so many people sitting around him listening to his music. That is his job in heaven," I continued. "He plays beautiful music for others."

David was at peace and was playing from his heart. It was such a beautiful sight to see, and I described it in detail for his beloved sister. David's sister just sat in her chair, completely amazed. She said David loved to play the guitar and that he was very good at it.

"His dream was for people to listen to him play," she said.

I guess his dream came true!

~The Addict's Gift of Song~

During another group reading, I connected with a mother who had passed at an early age. Her daughter had attended the reading just out of curiosity, and she was one of the first people to connect with a loved one. Her mother came in so gently and sweetly and began to show me a movie of her life. She had succumbed to the world of addiction and had chosen a path of self-destruction rather than a path of motherhood. She came through with such remorse and regret and asked her daughter for forgiveness. She spoke of her daughter's pregnancy and asked her daughter to put pictures of her up when her baby boy was born.

"Your son will recognize her," I told the young woman sitting in front of me. "She has kept him close to her until it was time for him to come."

The young woman's reading continued, and her mother acknowledged that she was having a boy.

"She says he's going to be a healing baby," I said. "He is coming to help others heal."

The young girl took it all in so gracefully. She said that everything I was saying made sense and that she had forgiven her mother long ago.

"I understand that you have already forgiven her, but it's important to let her say she is sorry," I said. "It will help your mother release the guilt she has been carrying."

As the reading progressed, I began to see the young woman's mother in heaven.

"Your mother is singing," I told her. "She has one of the most beautiful voices I've ever heard."

The young woman's eyes grew big, and she proceeded to tell the group that her mother had one of the most beautiful voices around.

"She wanted to be a professional singer," she said, "but then she started using drugs and she stopped singing."

I told the young woman that her mother's dream had finally come true. She was singing her heart out, and it was so beautiful.

"She's singing for everyone in heaven, and they absolutely love her voice."

I told the young woman to be open to the possibility that she might one day be able to hear her mother's voice from heaven. I hope and pray that she did.

Chapter 40

Fallen Angels

As I begin this chapter, I can't help but think that it may just be the most controversial of them all. As I stated at the beginning of this book, I didn't set out on this journey to convince anyone of anything. I merely answered a call within that became too strong to ignore. If I could help even just one person with my written words, then that would be reward enough. This chapter is about fallen angels and my astonishing personal experiences with them. I hope you can read about my personal accounts with an open mind and an open heart. You may just see things from a new perspective.

There are many references about fallen angels in the Bible. It is said that they are cast out of heaven after performing acts against God and that they are banished out of heaven and into hell, where they will remain for eternity. After doing this work for several years and having my own experiences with fallen angels, I can't help but wonder if we have all of the facts. If this subject makes you nervous, I completely understand. So many of us were taught certain things growing up, but I can assure you that this is a beautiful story with an ending that will fill your heart with love and joy. I would encourage you to read on.

I have had a number of experiences with fallen angels. Yes, they have been cast out of heaven to live their days here on earth. Living here on earth, as an angel who has been stripped of all love, light, and power, truly is hell for them. And just to clarify something: as I write this portion of my book, I will be referring to angels as male or female, as they sometimes exude a more masculine or feminine energy.

Throughout the past several years, I have encountered a handful of fallen angels. I believe that these fallen angels are what people have seen when they refer to seeing "demons." They appear a dark grayish-black in color and appear to have somewhat dried-up skin. Their eyes can be as black as coal or as red as fire, and I believe that it is our own beliefs and fears that will help manifest how they appear to us. They can appear so big and frightening, a far cry from the amazingly beautiful angels they once were. They are lost in a world that was not made for them, and they are so frightened of being discovered that they will go to any lengths to stay hidden. As far as I can tell, there are many, but they are not banded together like some sort of army. They exist alone, in complete fear and isolation. They exist among us and work desperately to instill fear in those around them, all to ensure that they will be left alone. Their energy is much different from that of humans whose souls haven't crossed over, as it feels much darker and more sinister. From what I have gathered in my many dealings with these fallen angels, their energy appears so negative because they were once such beautiful and loving beings, not of this world. To go from that space of love and light working as God's messengers to a place where the vibration just does not resonate with them shifts these angels in ways we could never imagine. Still yet, if you believe that everything was created by God, and in the likeness of God, you must believe that love can still exist even within these fallen angels.

Fallen angels feed on our fears. They relish in the fact that we fear even the thought of their existence. They know our weaknesses and prey upon them, with the intention of keeping us so scared that we would never dream of messing with them. I heard a story once of a gentleman who believed he had an encounter with one of these "demons." He was known to carry a rosary with him at all times, pulling it out often to say prayers of protection. He lived in fear and would say prayers morning and night. One evening, while he was at home, he began to feel a presence near him. He explained it as an evil presence, and he felt that he was in grave danger. He pulled out his rosary, and as he did, this "demon" grabbed it and tore it apart. When I was asked if I believed something like this was possible, I simply said yes. I do believe that these fallen angels can do scary and sometimes awful things if we believe that they can. Especially when we give them so much power. I'm certain there are many others who have had experiences similar to or possibly even worse than this gentleman's, and I hope the following story can help those individuals in some way.

~The Angel at the Top of the Stairs~

My first encounter with a fallen angel occurred after moving in with my boyfriend, Michael. I had lived in that little house at the lake, the one that I mentioned in the beginning of my book, for several years. It was time for a change, and Michael and I had been dating for some time, so we decided it was time to move in together. I sold my house and moved into his house with my two little dogs.

Michael's home would prove to be a place for learning even more about my abilities. It was the place where I would see my first full apparition, Mary, floating down the stairs. You may recall that story from earlier in my book as well. Well, Mary would only be the beginning of what I can describe as my "full awakening." The experience I shared with her would be the catalyst to many more amazing synchronicities and occurrences that would happen in my life. I had no idea of the capacity of my abilities, but I was on my way to experiencing things like never before.

I smudged our home with white sage regularly, clearing out any negative energy that may have crept its way in. Things always went smoothly, but I have to admit, I always felt like something was still there. I couldn't put my finger on it, but something didn't feel right. My dogs even acted different in Michael's home. Rosie would occasionally growl at Daisy, something she had never done before, and they began to have accidents in the house, something they had also never done before. I knew something wasn't right, but I just didn't know why.

I attended a spiritual retreat with my mentor one summer and was introduced to Palo Santo. I had never heard of it before, but my mentor just couldn't say enough good things about it.

"Palo Santo means 'Holy Stick,'" she told me, "and it is very powerful for clearing lower energy." I was intrigued, and when I got home, I ordered some. Within a few days, my Palo Santo had arrived.

I decided to give my new clearing stick a try. It was a Friday night and Michael was heading to the garage, his man cave, to have a beer and watch some television. I told him I would join him, but I wanted to clear the house first. I was eager to try the Palo Santo, as I had read that it was very powerful for not only clearing but for illuminating what, if anything, lies around us.

I began as I always did, by saying a prayer and calling in all of my helpers. I asked God to fill our home with light and called on Archangel Michael for protection. I called on all of the angels and archangels to help clear any lower energy that might be lurking within my home and lit the Palo Santo. I started in the basement, where I always did, moving about in a clockwise motion, envisioning the energy moving upward and outward. I made my way to the first floor, where I continued clearing with the Palo Santo and my favorite smudging feather. Everything was quite calm and moving along smoothly. Things certainly felt different. Lighter than usual. Maybe there was something to this "Holy Stick."

When I was finished with the first floor, I began moving up the stairs to the second floor. I'll never forget the feeling I felt as I started up the stairs. I had never felt it before. I was totally creeped out. I felt an uneasy feeling and it felt like something was lurking above me in the ceiling. There is a high ceiling above the staircase, and I could feel something peering down at me. I paused and allowed the vision to come in. It played in my mind like a movie and I began to see something dark in color, a dark grayish-black "something." It had wings, and its skin was all shriveled up. It was masculine energy, and I could see it plain as day. Needless to say, this freaked me out a little, as I had never encountered anything like this before. And I had cleared a lot of houses! I abruptly turned around and headed down the stairs, all the while saying, *What the hell was that?* over and over in my head. I set the Palo Santo down in my conch shell, laid down my smudging feather, and headed out the back door to the garage where Michael was.

When I walked into the garage, I sat across from where Michael was sitting. My face must have said it all because as soon as I sat down, his eyes got really big and he asked, "What in the heck did you see?"

All I could muster was a shaky, "I don't know." After a few moments I began telling him what happened and described the creature that I had seen. As I told Michael the story, his face began to shift into that of a look of surprise and disbelief.

"I can't believe you just said that," he said. He paused for a moment and then added, "I saw that thing ten years ago."

My response was quite funny, because all that I could come up with was, "Why didn't you tell me that before?" After an awkward silence, I just started laughing. I mean, you've got to admit it—we were having one crazy conversation. After a few more minutes, I had gained my composure and decided to head back inside. I sat up, stated my intentions, and marched back into the house.

"There is no way I'm going to share my home with something like that," I said fearlessly. "It has to go."

When I entered the house, I sat down on the couch and came to a place of deep connection. I felt calm and peaceful and knew that everything was going to be okay. I called on God and said, "God, creator of all that is, please show me what this is, and what I need to do."

There was no hesitation in His answer, and I heard it clearly. "Fallen angel."

Whoa, I thought. "That is crazy," I said out loud. Things started going through my head, things that I had been taught as a young girl, such as, "angels who are cast out of heaven can never return." Well, if that was the case, so be it, but this thing was not going to live in the same house that I lived in. I closed my eyes once again and asked God to shine His light brighter than ever. I called on Jesus and Archangel Michael and asked for their help.

"Please help me with this fallen angel," I prayed.

As soon as I had asked, Jesus and Archangel Michael arrived. And like so many times before, that movie began to play in my head. I saw

Jesus and Archangel Michael walking toward the fallen angel, who was hiding in the stairwell. The angel was weeping uncontrollably and shaking in complete fear, and I watched as it pulled itself up into a tight, little ball in the corner of the ceiling as Jesus and Archangel Michael approached. While I watched, I was guided to ask Jesus to place His hands upon the angel, which He did so lovingly. I watched as the angel immediately began to calm down. The angel's tears began to stop and he looked at Jesus's loving eyes. With His hands still upon the angel's shoulders, Jesus said, "My father forgives everyone. All you have to do is ask. It's time to come home."

The vision continued, and I watched as Jesus walked toward the light with His arm around the angel. Archangel Michael walked on the other side of the angel, ensuring him that everything was going to be okay.

"We've missed you," I heard Archangel Michael say to him as they made their way to the light. As soon as they all entered the light, the fallen angel turned into the beautiful angel that he was before. He floated up, looking up at the bright light coming from above. It was if I could hear God talking to him, telling him how much He loved him.

"Welcome home," was His greeting.

As the angel reached the bright lights of heaven, my vision was over. I sat weeping for a bit, not out of sadness, but rather from a sense of joy. It was one of the most beautiful and loving things I had ever experienced, and my heart felt so full. After a few moments, I got up and finished clearing the rest of the house, as I wanted to ensure that I cleared any residual energy that might have been left by the fallen angel. As I finished clearing, I could see the angel looking down from heaven at me. Although his lips weren't actually moving, I could hear him talking to me. He was thanking me for helping him get home, and he promised to watch over me forever.

"I will bring you many blessings," I heard him say. He was so grateful, and I could feel the love he held for me.

"You're welcome, sweet angel," I said quietly. "Thank you for my lesson."

I thanked him for all that he had taught me that day, and I thanked God, Jesus, and Archangel Michael for helping me see the truth. My experience with that fallen angel taught me lots of things, but most importantly that God loves us unconditionally and wants us all to come home.

I have had just a few experiences with fallen angels. Several of my students report that they have encountered them as well. They always report an easy transition for these fallen angels when calling upon God, Jesus, and Archangel Michael for help. Here's just one more beautiful story about another fallen angel making its way home.

~Archangel Michael's Right-Hand Angel~

I received a call late one evening from one of my clients who had ended up becoming a close and dear friend. She was calling rather late, around nine-thirty in the evening, so I answered the phone knowing that it must be something important.

"I'm so sorry to call so late, but I just have to ask you something," Robin said.

I quickly put her at ease and asked her what was going on. Robin proceeded to tell me that she had been experiencing a very eerie feeling, something that had been occurring for quite some time. She said she had always had a feeling like something was watching her, and this feeling was something that she had felt in her old home as well as her brand-new home, which she and her husband had just built the year before. "I thought the feeling would go away when we moved, but I just feel like something has been following me all of these years," Robin said, "and it's not a good feeling."

Robin had always been sensitive and had even taken my mediumship course, so she was pretty right on when it came to things like this. As she continued, she explained that she was rarely able to sleep through the night and would often wake up feeling like something was watching her. As she talked, I began to get a sense of the negative energy that was in her home. It was a different feeling than I normally get when dealing with spirits who have not yet crossed into the light, but I wasn't able to get a clear picture of what it was just yet. Although I didn't quite know what it was, I felt a very uneasy feeling and knew that it definitely needed to go. I didn't want to frighten or alarm Robin and asked her if we could do a prayer right then and there, calling in all of her guides and angels, to help clear the energy from her home. Robin agreed, so I called on God and asked Him to put his light in and around Robin's home and asked Him to shine it so bright. I called on Jesus and Archangel Michael to help clear anything that was of lower energy, ensuring a quick and easy passage into the light. I called on Archangel Michael and asked him to surround Robin, her husband, and all of their animals with protection so that they could have a restful night sleeping.

"All is well," I told her. "When you wake tomorrow, everything will feel different."

Robin thanked me and we ended the call. I still had an uneasy feeling and felt that things weren't completely finished yet, but I wasn't sure why. I asked for any further guidance on Robin's situation and remained open to what I might receive.

I went to bed that evening and fell fast asleep. I was sleeping quite soundly when I suddenly awoke in the middle of the night. It was as if I was lying on Robin's bed, looking up at her ceiling. I saw it, that presence hanging in her ceiling, and recognized it immediately. It was a fallen angel. I saw as it hid in the corner of her ceiling, near her bathroom, when she and her husband were awake. At night, it would just lurk above them, instilling an uneasy feeling and sometimes fear in Robin and her husband. I saw what it was doing, and I was going to put a stop to it.

Oh, no, you don't, I exclaimed, in my head, of course, as my boyfriend was sleeping right next to me. I called on God and commanded that He shine His light into Robin's home, directly into her bedroom. I called on Jesus and Archangel Michael and commanded them to go to the fallen angel as it hid, shaking there in the corner. The angel was terrified, as it knew it had been discovered. As I watched the movie unfold inside my head, I watched as Archangel Michael went over to the fallen angel and placed his hand on his shoulder. It was if they knew each other on a deeper level and had been quite close at one time. I watched as Archangel Michael stood on one side of the angel and Jesus on the other. They walked with him toward the light, and as they did, I could feel the huge burden of remorse and shame the angel had been carrying. Although I never got the exact reason for the angel being cast out of heaven, I did get a sense of how very sorry he was.

The angel wept uncontrollably as they walked toward the light. He was so broken and weary. He had been here for a very long time—here in an energy that was so foreign to his own, and now it was time to go home. As soon as Jesus, Archangel Michael, and the fallen angel reached the beam of white light, the angel instantly began to float upward toward heaven. I watched as he shifted into a beautiful light-blue color as he was being filled up with love and light once again. A smile came over his face as he floated upward and saw God waiting to welcome him home. I began to hear the conversation that was going on between all of them and began to get a clearer picture of who this fallen angel really was. This angel, who had been cast out from heaven so long ago, was Archangel Michael's right-hand man, or angel, in this case. I'm not sure what he had done to be cast out, but I knew it was a big deal. He had played an important role as Archangel Michael's soldier, if you will, and he had been deeply missed. He stood next to Archangel Michael now, ready to serve with him once again. The angel thanked me for all I had done and left me with a loving message. "I will be watching over you now, and you can expect many blessings, as I will work diligently to make sure you are showered with them." I felt such gratitude coming from the angel, and I knew that he would be watching over me and helping me from this point on.

When I awoke the next morning, I couldn't wait to talk to Robin. I didn't want to freak her out with everything that had happened until I knew that things felt better in her home. I dialed her number and she quickly answered.

"How'd you sleep last night?" I asked.

She replied by saying that it had been the best night of sleep she had had in a very long time.

"Julia, I slept through the whole night. I can't remember that last time I did that."

I felt relieved and then proceeded to tell her what had happened. I told her how I had connected with the fallen angel and told her everything that had occurred the night before. I told her every last detail and assured her that her home felt completely clear now.

"I didn't want to alarm you last night, but I really didn't know what it was. I felt something was definitely there, watching you, but I didn't want to worry you until I knew exactly what it was," I explained. Robin said that she felt different when she woke that morning and that the house felt so different.

"I didn't have that creepy feeling today like I always do. It felt good," Robin said.

Thank goodness, I thought to myself. It had worked. Robin was free and another angel had made it back home.

I speak with Robin periodically, and she reports that her home feels so pleasant. She hasn't felt that uneasy, creepy feeling that she experienced for so many years since I helped remove the fallen angel. Her husband even reports a change in the house, saying that he, too, felt a creepy feeling in their home once they were married and sharing space together. All is well, and they are enjoying their new life together.

Chapter 41

Dreams

Our loved ones, angels, and guides often come in our dreams. For many of us, it is the only time we are still and not thinking about our next step. Our minds are quiet, which allows for other things to enter, and often it is a time that our loved ones, angels, and guides can offer us much-needed support and guidance.

I often receive visits from angels and guides while I sleep. I remember one time in particular when I was shaken awake in the middle of the night. I woke to the feeling that someone was shaking me. I mean, someone literally had a hold of my shoulders and was shaking me hard. My head, shoulders, and chest were even coming up off of the bed. Now, I can see where most people would completely freak out and think that something evil or sinister was behind it all, but by the time this had happened to me, I was in a place where I knew better than to jump to any conclusions. I lay back down and got into my zone. I connected with God and asked what this was all about.

Who is this? I demanded. I said this inside my head, of course, as Michael was sleeping quite soundly right beside me. As soon as I had asked, I heard my answer.

Archangel Michael.

I was puzzled for just a moment, as I found it hard to believe that this loving angel would've shaken me like that.

Why did you do that? I asked. Archangel Michael's answer was swift and firm.

You are not paying attention, he said boldly. *You are ignoring the signs.*

As soon as I heard his words, I knew exactly what he was talking about. I had been going through some difficult things and was dragging my feet in making some decisions. And he was right, I had been receiving the guidance I had asked for, only to ignore all of it and keep pushing through the darkness. I knew that shaking me while I slept was probably just what I needed; he'd been trying to get my attention for so long.

Okay, okay, I answered. *But please, don't ever do that again.* With that, I drifted back to sleep.

The next morning, I finally took the advice that the angels had been giving me. I knew what I needed to do, and I put my foot forward. I made those very difficult decisions and trusted that my angels and guides would take care of everything. They would prove to me once again that they were working in my favor. Those decisions I finally found the courage to make turned out to be some of the best decisions of my life.

***

Here's another story about a woman who dreamt of her mother after her passing. Her experience was much different from mine, but you will see that what happened in her dream was a huge lesson for her as well.

~Linda~

I met with a woman who wanted to connect with family members in heaven. She had lost so many loved ones, and the grief she felt inside showed heavily upon her face. Linda had lost several family members, and as her reading began, they wasted no time coming in to say hello. They were so eager to connect with her and let her know they were with her. When Linda arrived at my home, she looked weary and sad. Although she entered with a huge grin, I could see and feel the intense grief and sadness that lay beneath her painted smile.

Linda's reading moved at a brisk pace. She heard from her father, mother, several aunts and uncles, and even grandparents. We both experienced amazing things during her reading. We had chills all through our bodies as we connected with Linda's mother and a dear friend, and I explained to Linda that these chills were her loved one's energy with us at that very moment. Even as I told her that, the chills became more and more intense. I always try to help my clients tune into their own bodies and become aware of their own signs. I told Linda to pay attention any time she called on her mother, or any of her loved ones, to see if she got the chills. This would be her sign that they were near and that they had heard her call.

"Now, that doesn't mean that if you call on them and feel nothing that they aren't there," I clarified. "It just means that you may feel more intense energy once in awhile."

As Linda's reading neared the end, I asked her if she had seen her mother since her passing. Linda's face began to tremble and tears started to well up in her eyes as she told me she had had a dream about her mother. In the dream, her mother had come to her

"She was standing there in front of me, asking me how I could've let her die," she said while choking back tears. As I tuned in to Linda's mother, I told Linda that she did, in fact, see her mother, but that her own guilt had swayed the conversation.

"Your mother said that she came to tell you what really happened, but when you saw her, your guilt took over, and all you heard was that you had let her die," I told her. Linda's mother went into great detail, and I told her that her mother had actually been spared a very agonizing and painful death.

"She says that she died because of some sort of fluke accident or something."

Linda began to fill me in; her mother had gone in for a routine surgery to repair a hiatal hernia. There were complications after her surgery, which ultimately caused her death.

"Something was brewing in her stomach area, and it wasn't going to be a peaceful ending," I continued. "No one knew about it yet, but it wasn't going to be pretty."

About that time, I saw Linda's father come into the picture. He was pleading with God and asking Him to spare his wife the pain of going through the horrible cancer that was lurking inside.

"Your father asked God to bring her home," I told her as she began to cry. When she was able, Linda asked if her mother knew she had cancer.

"No, she didn't know," I replied. "What you thought was a botched surgery actually saved her from suffering a horrible death. Your mother wants you to know that it was actually a blessing, and she wants you to let go of any guilt you still have over the whole thing. She assures you that there was nothing you could've done."

Linda let out a big sigh of relief through her tears. It was apparent that she had been carrying this heavy load for quite some time. Linda's reading came to an end and we thanked our angels and guides for being with us. Linda thanked her father for taking care of her mother and thanked her mom for helping her let go of her guilt. In just a short sixty minutes, Linda's demeanor had completely changed. She looked brighter and her eyes sparkled a bit as she let out a huge smile.

"You have no idea how much you've helped me today," Linda said as she leaned in for a hug. I could feel the gratitude pouring out from her heart, but I was grateful too—grateful for the opportunity to witness another broken soul step into the light. I can only imagine that Linda's life began to shift in miraculous ways after her reading. She was finally rid of the burden of guilt she had carried since her mother's passing, and she could rest easy knowing that her mother and father were together once again.

Chapter 42

The Panels of Retribution

I certainly couldn't let this book be complete without talking about the panels of retribution. These are the panels that souls who did bad things to others here on earth without showing any remorse must face. Some people do unspeakable things, and I have all too often connected with these souls while doing readings for those they hurt.

The degree of pain and suffering these individuals have caused varies from situation to situation. But please know that they did not get off scot-free. The panels of retribution are nothing short of payback, as departed souls must not only watch a movie of their life but must feel the pain and suffering, on an emotional level, that they inflicted on their victims.

The panels are made up of three and appear smoky-colored. Souls are placed in front of them, generally sitting, where they must watch an entire movie of their lives. The panels are just outside of that golden door that opens up to heaven, and Archangel Michael stands watch diligently until each movie has come to an end. I have done numerous readings where I have seen the panels, but one reading in particular has always stuck with me, whether I wanted it to or not.

I've decided not to go into the horrific details of how my client was abused by her father, but I can honestly say that what he did was beyond reprehensible. As I began Grace's reading, I saw all of the horrible things her father had done to her when she was young. I was reluctant to tell her what I was seeing but knew that I was receiving guidance that would help her, as I always asked for that during my opening prayer. I told Grace what I saw and she validated that it was indeed true. The reading continued, and the details of Grace's tormented and tortured childhood just got worse. I couldn't believe how much she had been through and that she had come out of it all such a beautiful spirit.

"Your dad is sitting in front of three panels," I told Grace. "He is watching a movie about his life. He must sit and watch and feel all of the emotional pain he caused you and everyone else. Archangel Michael is standing there, guarding the door, and making certain that he watches it to the very end."

Grace's eyes filled with tears, and they began to flow down her rosy cheeks as I continued.

"Your father is sobbing," I told her. "He can't believe all the pain he caused."

We sat there holding hands for a few moments as I continued telling Grace what I was seeing. "I've never seen anyone cry like that," I said. "He had to sit there for thirteen days."

Now, I know that thirteen days to you and I doesn't sound like very long, but I can assure you that it is a very long time up there. I felt the magnitude of the time that Grace's father had to sit in front of those panels, and I'll have to admit, I felt a little sorry for him. Grace did too. As her tears began to stop, she simply said, "I hope they let him into heaven."

My heart went out to this beautiful earth angel sitting across from me as I validated that he was eventually let in.

"Archangel Michael let him in when he was finished watching his movie," I assured her. "Your father is so sorry for everything he did to you. He is begging for your forgiveness."

Grace nodded her head and said, "I forgave him a long time ago."

I learned so much from Grace's reading. It was the first reading I had done where I was able to see the panels. Since then, I have done many more where I am able to see souls sitting in front of them, watching their own movies and learning their own lessons. Times seem to vary from a few days to several. To date, Grace's father had to sit the longest. Grace literally graced my life. She had been through so much in her lifetime, much more than her fair share, and yet, she was still able to forgive her father for all that he had done. Grace is a beautiful light, and I can only hope that I can be as loving and forgiving as she. Thank you, Grace, for being one of my most important teachers. God bless.

And now, on to one of my favorite subjects: angels.

Chapter 43

Archangel Michael

Although there are so many angels and archangels who are available to us, I felt guided to talk specifically about Archangel Michael, our beloved protector. Archangel Michael is my "go-to" angel whenever I feel vulnerable or afraid and need a boost of courage and strength. He comes to us immediately, the second we call on him, and is ready to help each and every one of us at any time. He is able to be with many people at the same time, so don't ever feel that you are taking him away from someone else. But be sure to call on him, as he is not allowed to help us unless we do. God created the angels that way. They aren't allowed to interfere with free will and must wait for us to call for help.

Archangel Michael shows up in many different ways. For some, they might feel a sense of warmth come over their bodies, while others may see the color purple or blue sparkles. He is tall and strong and can handle anything we throw at him. He generally comes as gentle, yet strong energy, but he may need to be a bit more forceful, especially if you've been asking him for help or guidance and for some reason or another, you are unable to receive that which he is sending to you. Remember the story about him shaking me awake in the middle of the night? Archangel Michael doesn't mess around!

I have worked with several families who are raising children who have the ability to see or sense spirit energy. Sometimes these youngsters are fearful of what is happening around them. They sometimes get caught up in a negative and scary place and don't know where to turn for help. Parents often feel helpless, not knowing if what their children are experiencing is real or just their imagination. Children who have the ability to connect with spirit often grow up living a life of confusion, doubt, and fear, as those around them may not understand what they are going through. One of the best pieces of advice I can offer parents of a child who reports seeing, hearing, or sensing "monsters," "people," or "spirits" is to just be open to the possibility that it could actually be happening. Your child may, in fact, be experiencing things that you're just not meant to. I always think about the children who come running to their moms and dads with reports of "seeing a monster," only to be told, "There's nothing in your room. Now go back to bed." How scary is that?!

When working with families of sensitive children, my first piece of advice is to begin telling them about Archangel Michael. I always suggest that parents find a picture of Archangel Michael that their child likes and post it above his or her bed. All one needs to do is to Google Archangel Michael's name and hundreds of photographs will pop up. And many of them are free! I encourage parents to begin a nightly routine of sitting with their child and either praying to Archangel Michael or simply asking him to watch over them as they sleep. I often suggest helping younger children envision Archangel Michael wrapping his purple cape around them as they sleep as well as in the morning as they get ready to go to school. Archangel Michael loves all of us and wants to help ease our fears. He loves your children dearly and is always ready to stand watch over them, helping them along their journey as they learn the lessons they were sent here to learn. Call on him to watch over all of you, as he can be with each and every one of us at the same time.

Archangel Michael can help with so much more. He is one of the angels that I call in when clearing my own home or when clearing the homes of others. I call him in to protect everyone during the clearing and ask him to round up any lower energies that need to go to the light. He also helps us cut cords to people, places, and past events that often hold us hostage and keep us from moving forward. Just sit quietly, close your eyes, and ask him to take his mighty sword and cut any unwanted cords. You just may feel an instant shift as he separates you from all of the garbage you've unknowingly absorbed from others. Archangel Michael offers us courage and strength as we continue on our journey. No job is too big or too small. All we need to do is ask.

The next story is about an encounter that several of my friends and I had with Archangel Michael while visiting a spiritual retreat in Sedona, Arizona. Although we felt completely surrounded by all of the angels during our stay, our encounter with Archangel Michael was quite amazing.

~Archangel Michael's Mountain~

I spoke about a trip that I took to Sedona, Arizona, at the beginning of this book. It was a life-changing event that helped me begin my journey toward the light. One thing that happened during that week was an encounter with Archangel Michael. There were several mountains that surrounded the valley where we stayed—four, to be exact—each named after one of the archangels. One mountain in particular was quite close to the cabin I had been assigned to, and I hiked it daily. It was called Archangel Michael's Mountain, and it was a majestic mountain with steep slopes and a flat peak on the top. Many of us from the group would make our way to the mountain daily, crossing a small bridge that guided us over a rapid stream. We would sit in meditation on the many rock formations that formed shelves within the mountain's steep slopes. I could feel Archangel Michael's energy so strongly as I sat in silence. He filled me with such a warm feeling and made me feel so loved and protected.

As our time in Sedona was coming to a close, we began taking several pictures of the various mountains that surrounded us. I wanted one of Archangel Michael's Mountain to add to my scrapbook, as I wanted to be able to recall the amazing connection I felt while sitting on that mountain. I thanked Archangel Michael for remaining so close to me during my time in Sedona. I had gone there to heal and knew that he was instrumental in the healing that had taken place. I was sad to leave that magical place but knew that I would someday return to sit with him again on his majestic mountain.

When I returned home from my trip, I began to look through all of the photos that many of us had shared with one another. One of the girls had sent a picture of Archangel Michael's Mountain with a caption that read, "You're not going to believe this." I opened the attachment and couldn't believe my eyes. The picture was of that majestic mountain we had all spent so much time walking and sitting upon, but in front of the mountain was a picture of Archangel Michael himself! He came as a huge, purple hue in front of the mountain, and I could even make out what appeared to be his wings. How amazing that Archangel Michael was able to let us know that he had been with us the whole time. I was grateful that he gave us this concrete sign and knew that if he could do that, he could do anything.

I have included the picture of Archangel Michael's Mountain. It might help to know that the purple hue didn't show up until the picture was uploaded to the computer. We had no idea it was even there until we began reviewing pictures from our magical pilgrimage. Thank you, Archangel Michael!

Although black and white doesn't do this photo justice, you can still make out the outline of Archangel Michael in front of the mountain. Just imagine it in brilliant purple!

Chapter 44

Guardian Angels

We all have guardian angels. They have been with us since birth. We may have one or two or several hundred who watch over us. I always joke that I must have hundreds of them, as that is surely the only way I made it through my teen years. Although you may have several guardian angels watching over you, there is one who acts as the main guardian angel. I often see this guardian angel when sitting with clients for readings, and many clients share that they are able to feel their guardian angels around them from time to time.

Our guardian angels love us unconditionally and are always by our sides, and although these angels are all ours, they are not allowed to help us unless we ask them to. God doesn't allow them to interfere with our own free will, so it is imperative that you call on them each and every day. Our angels wait eagerly for us to call on them, as they have ways of helping us that we may not even fathom. The only time that God allows our guardian angels to intervene without us calling on them is if we are involved in a life-or-death situation and it's not our time to die. Then, and only then, are they allowed to step in and take over.

Your guardian angels want you to know them. They each have names and different personalities and may sometimes feel more masculine or feminine, or a combination of the two. Each guardian angel has its own unique name and just loves to reveal them to us when we are ready. I learned the name of one of my guardian angels several years ago, when I was attending a class where the teacher guided us into meditation where we would be connecting with our guardian angels. The intention of the meditation was to hear one of our angel's names. I recall being so excited about this particular class, as I had been studying the angels for quite some time and could feel their presence around me often. The teacher began taking us on a journey where we were guided into a very relaxed state. Although I can't remember the details of the meditation, as it was so many years ago, I will never forget hearing a name so crystal-clear. Ariel. She spoke so lovingly as she told me her name. *What a beautiful name,* I thought. Her energy was nurturing and kind, and I could feel the love that she had for me. As the meditation ended and we were guided back into a place of awareness, our guide told us to continue to talk with our guardian angels often. She said that we would begin to see our angel's name everywhere as validation that we had heard the name correctly. As I left that evening, I asked Ariel to continue to show me that she was around and that I would be open to however she wanted to do that.

The very next day, I was traveling down the interstate making my way to my morning yoga class. As I was preparing to take the exit that would take me to my class, a huge semi truck came barreling along beside me. Written in bold, red letters was "Ariel Trucking." I couldn't believe it! It was Ariel letting me know that that was indeed her name and that she was right there with me. And if that wasn't enough, just a few short days later, I was reading a book that I had been thoroughly enjoying for several days. For the life of me, I can't recall the name of it, but I do remember that the author began talking about an imaginary friend she had as a child named ... you guessed it, Ariel!

Since learning Ariel's name, I have connected with several other guardian angels, including Seraphim and Joseph. I was so amazed with that initial guided meditation that had helped me connect with Ariel and learn her name that I decided to begin offering a class and guided meditation of my own aimed at doing the same thing. I wanted to help others gain a stronger connection with their guardian angels, just as I had.

During one of my classes, I led a small group into a guided meditation. After helping the group get into a deep state of relaxation,

I led them into the angels' crystal palace. This is a magical place full of so many different crystals and vibrant colors. I told the group to envision the crystal palace and to get a sense of all of the love that was inside of those magic walls. I asked for all of their guardian angels to step forward and instructed the group to ask at least one of their guardian angel's names.

"Just be open to whatever you hear," I told them. The intention was to hear at least one of their angel's names, but I left it open to however many angels wanted to come forward.

"You might hear one and you might hear several," I continued. "Whatever it is, ii's perfect for you."

When the meditation was over and I had brought the group back into complete awareness of the present time and space, I asked if everyone had heard a name. As I looked around the room, just about everyone was nodding their head yes, but there was one woman who shrugged her shoulders. She looked unsure of what had happened, and I could see the disappointment on her face. I addressed the group and told them that angels don't always have angelic-sounding names.

"The name could even be Tommy," I said. As soon as I said the name, that woman's eyes just got as big as could be. I mean, her face was priceless! The woman spoke up and said that she couldn't believe that I had just said that name. As she spoke, she turned the piece of paper around that she had been writing on. She had written down her angel's name on a piece of paper, as I had encouraged everyone to do. She turned the piece of paper around where we could all see it, and in big, bold letters, she had written the name Tommy. Needless to say, we all got a laugh out of that one.

I just love how Tommy came through with the validation that this woman needed. She doubted her angel's name, but he managed to come through with validation that it truly was him. I can't help but feel that she knew she was indeed being watched over by her guardian angel, Tommy.

Chapter 45

How They Connect with Us

I continue to be amazed at the miraculous ways that our loved ones, angels, and guides are able to connect with us. The possibilities are truly unlimited. They can come in quite unique and surprising ways if we allow ourselves to be open to infinite possibilities. They can send feathers and coins, rainbows, and even faces in the clouds. They can even show up as a butterfly, as one client's beloved dog, Indy, did.

I was doing a reading for a young girl named Jaden. She wanted desperately to connect with her dog Indy, who had passed a few years before. I told her that Indy came as an orange butterfly. As we walked out of my house where Jaden's mother had been waiting in the car, her mother stood outside with her camera yelling, "Hey, come look at this orange butterfly. It's has been flying around me this entire time!"

They might come as a particular scent, perhaps of a favorite cologne, the smell of flowers, or a smelly old football jersey. You might even smell cigarette or cigar smoke when they are near, letting you know that they are still watching over everything. They might come as an orb in a picture or a sparkle of light that catches your glimpse for a brief moment. Some signs might be subtle, while others are placed right in plain view. I remember back when I was getting a reading with my mentor one time. Jackie mentioned that there was a hummingbird there with her and that it had shown up much earlier than it usually did. We both knew why it had come at that exact moment, as she had just been telling me that my life was beginning to get filled up with so much joy. The hummingbird is a sign for that—that more joy is coming your way.

Anyway, Jackie said something like, "Oh, there he goes," explaining that the hummingbird had just flown away. As soon as she had uttered the last word, a hummingbird landed on my feeder at my back door. We laughed as we realized that there just was no end to the magic that they could make happen.

Some people have specific signs that they get over and over from their beings of light to let them know they're on the right path and that they are being guided every step of the way. For me, my sign is hearts. I mean, I find them everywhere. I find heart rocks almost daily, and I have collected hundreds over the years. I finally had to stop picking them up because I was running out of places to put them. Sometimes, if I need a little pick-me-up, I ask the angels for a sign and say something like, "I'd like to find a heart rock today." Before you know it, I've stumbled across one. But rocks aren't the only way I receive my heart messages. One day, on a cold and blistery winter morning, I walked along the river that runs behind my house. I was taking pictures of some of the beautiful icicles that formed along the river's edge when suddenly, I felt the presence of fairies. I asked the fairies to give me a sign that they were there as I bent down to take a picture of some icicles. After returning home and uploading my pictures to my computer, I'm sure you can imagine my surprise when I saw a heartcicle, which is what I like to call what's in the picture below.

And it doesn't stop there! I find hearts everywhere. And by everywhere, I mean everywhere. One even showed up in my eggs when I was getting ready to make French toast. When I texted the picture to my mom, she jokingly replied, "What kind of chickens do you have there in Pennsylvania?"

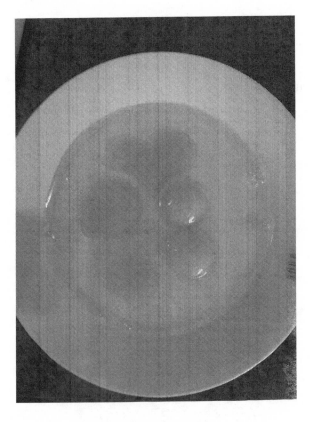

We can receive signs in so many ways that are not limited to what I have included in this book. Your loved ones, angels, and guides may have their very own unique ways of connecting with you. Please know that when you "get that feeling," it is your loved one reaching out to you, letting you know that he or she is near. Our loved ones, angels, and guides want desperately to make things easier for us and wait patiently to hear what it is that we need. Talk to them often, and trust that they can hear everything. Tell them what you want and ask them for help, and they will answer your call. Ask them to give you signs, and be open to all of the ways they can come. Step into the light and into the flow of divine magic. And then, my friend, get ready for miracles.

Here are just a few more photos of the many hearts I've found over the years. Every time I find one, I'm reminded that I am not alone. My loved ones, angels, and guides are just letting me know that they love me unconditionally and that they are always by my side. Enjoy!

Found this heart on the wall of the groomer's place.
She didn't even know it was there until I pointed it out.

Found this one in the garden.

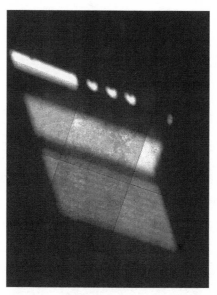

The sun was shining in my kitchen window. It took me awhile to figure it out, but I realized that the hearts were coming through the dish drain. (There are no hearts on the dish drain—lol.)

Found this lovely pear heart while walking along the river behind my house.

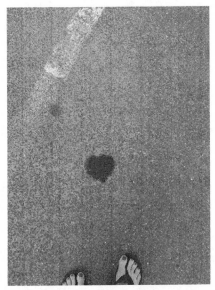

I noticed this oil stain walking to
my car after doing some shopping.

Heart cloud!

Getting ready for dinner and noticed
the light reflecting in my bowl.

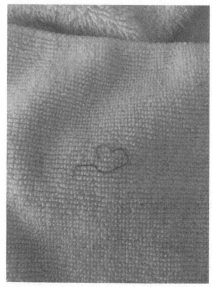

Found this one while folding towels.

A cute, little basil heart on my pizza

Hearts at dinner

While hiking

Noticed this little baby heart while heating up
some leftover yams and turnips.

I found this tiny heart inside of a bag that held a loaf of bread.

Raisin heart

Dehydrated-apple heart

Heart rock

Bagel heart

Tree-trunk heart

Found all of these on a thirty-minute walk.

Tea-bag heart

Just a few of my heart rocks that line my fence

Additional Resources

Phoenix Rizing Stables in Harvey's Lake, Pennsylvania:
E-mail Corey Snedden at Bumble2810@hotmail.com

43310475R00149

Made in the USA
Lexington, KY
27 July 2015